WARS OF
THE INTERIOR

WARS OF THE INTERIOR

JOSEPH ZÁRATE

Translated from the Spanish by Annie McDermott

GRANTA

Granta Publications, 12 Addison Avenue, London W11 4QR

First published in Great Britain by Granta Books, 2021

Copyright © 2018, Penguin Random House Grupo Editorial S. A.
Avenida Ricardo Palma 341, Oficina 504, Miraflores, Lima, Perú

English translation copyright © 2021, Annie McDermott

Originally published in 2018 as *Guerras del interior* by Debate,
Penguin Random House Grupo Editorial S. A., Lima

References to websites were correct at the time of writing.
A CIP catalogue record for this book is available from the British Library

9 8 7 6 5 4 3 2 1

ISBN 978 1 78378 615 2
eISBN 978 1 78378 616 9

www.granta.com

Typeset in Garamond by Avon DataSet Ltd, Arden Court,
Alcester, Warwickshire
Printed and bound by CPI Group (UK) Ltd, Croydon, CR0 4YY

In memory of Lilí Tuanama Núñez, my maternal grandmother, and of Vistoso, a vanished community in the Peruvian rainforest, where she was born and to which she could never return.

To Violeta and Pepe, my parents, every single one of my words.

CONTENTS

'What happens to great events? They migrate into history, while the little ones, the ones that are most important for the little person, disappear without a trace. [. . .] I strive desperately (from book to book) to do one and the same thing – reduce history to the human being.'

Svetlana Alexievich
Boys in Zinc

WOOD

'Our world is falling apart quietly. Human civilization has reduced the plant, a four-million-year-old life form, into three things: food, medicine, and wood. In our relentless and ever-intensifying obsession with obtaining a higher volume, potency, and variety of these three things, we have devastated plant ecology to an extent that millions of years of natural disaster could not.'

Hope Jahren
Lab Girl

'Seen from the air, the jungle below looked like kinky hair, seemingly peaceful, but that is deceptive, because in its inner being nature is never peaceful. Even when it is denatured, when it is tamed, it strikes back at its tamers and reduces them to pets.'

Werner Herzog
Conquest of the Useless

'And above all, you hear the sound of the steps of animals one has been before being human, the steps of the stones and the vegetables and the things every human being has previously been. And also what he has heard before, all of that you can hear at night in the jungle.'

César Calvo
The Three Halves of Ino Moxo: Teachings of the Wizard of the Upper Amazon

Those who knew him say that Edwin Chota had a broad, exaggerated, infectious grin, with a gap where he was missing a front tooth. His father, Alberto Chota Tenazoa, describes how, two years before the eldest of his six children was killed, Edwin Chota lost that tooth while tucking into a plate of turtle spaghetti. 'He bit into a piece of shell,' the old man recalls, 'but he just laughed, threw the tooth away and carried on eating.' The Asháninka hunter Jaime Arévalo, a member of the most populous indigenous nation in the Peruvian rainforest, remembered that missing tooth when he unearthed his friend's skull. He and some police officers had spent all morning dredging a pit of brown water near the border with Brazil. Edwin Chota's body had been dragged there by the river, and almost entirely devoured by vultures and alligators along the way. The pit was seven metres deep. Arévalo – a short man in his forties, a good swimmer with strong arms – pulled from it a femur, some ribs, a shirt torn to shreds, a rubber boot with holes in it and a bracelet made of colourful seeds, still attached to the wrist. Two weeks previously, four of Arévalo's friends had been murdered and then left in a nearby stream. These were the remains of one of them, as confirmed by a single detail: the skull was missing a tooth.

Despite being fifty-three years old and thin as a rake, Edwin Chota was a tenacious farmer and a skilled hunter with a shotgun. He had a pointed nose like an eagle, hair without a hint of grey and sun-toasted skin. He could mimic a sparrow's song or a wildcat's roar, was good at football, and danced huaynos by Sósimo Sacramento and Brazilian forró, moving his scrawny body like a puppet. When Edwin Chota smiled, that missing tooth, the upper right incisor, was the most noticeable thing about his face. And it was the same when he protested, although he didn't smile then. As the chief of Saweto, an Amazon community of more than thirty families on the Alto Tamaya river, Chota – the only adult there who could read and write – would rage and shake his fists when he denounced the log traffickers who exploited the Asháninka people, plundering the forest where they lived. 'It was the only time he was serious,' says Julia Pérez, his widow. 'The rest of the time he was a joker.' Smiling can sometimes be an act of diplomacy, but Chota never curved his lips when faced with an illegal logger.

To reach Pucallpa, the second-largest city in the Peruvian rainforest, where he was born and raised, Edwin Chota had to travel by boat for seven days down a winding river. He used to go there to see his father and bring him motelo, a kind of turtle with yellow feet and delicious, tender flesh, which had become the older man's favourite food. The last time they saw each other, on Father's Day, Chota told him he was going to Lima to see if someone would finally listen to his complaints. The death threats were becoming more and more frequent. His father begged him to stay in Pucallpa with him instead of returning to Saweto.

'I can't,' he said. 'I'll only leave that place when I'm dead.'

Two months later, on the morning of 1 September 2014, some loggers murdered Edwin Chota and three other Asháninka leaders – Jorge Ríos, Francisco Pinedo and Leoncio Quintisima – in the Alto Tamaya rainforest. They were on their way to a meeting on the Brazilian side of the border, to plan how to defend their territories. A bullet from a sixteen-gauge shotgun, designed for hunting deer and wild monkeys, went straight through Chota's chest. Another made a hole in his head. Arévalo the hunter, who'd set off ahead of them for the meeting, retraced his steps down the same path when he noticed that his friends hadn't arrived. Five days later he found the bodies in a stream, a twelve-hour walk from the border – afterwards, returning with the police, he would find only bones – and fled to his community, afraid of being killed as well. The four widows and the leaders' children travelled by boat for three days non-stop to Pucallpa, to report what had happened. There are no police in Saweto, and the two-channel radio the community owns – their only contact with the outside world – doesn't work very well.

The last time Edwin Chota went to Lima to report the loggers who were threatening him, he called his eighty-year-old father on his mobile and promised to visit. Some time before, he'd left him a photo as a memento: it showed Chota at one of the many meetings he attended as Asháninka chief, on his feet, unsmiling, in a cushma – a brown ankle-length tunic – and a multi-coloured feather headdress, his face painted with red stripes of achiote.[1] 'So if anything ever happens to me, you'll still be able to see me,' he told his dad, just before saying goodbye.

The man who died for the Saweto Asháninka community hadn't always been an Asháninka. When people told Perla Chota, his oldest daughter, that her father was the leader of

1 Achiote (*Bixa orellana*) is a tropical shrub that's very plentiful in the Peruvian Amazon, as well as in Brazil and Mexico. Its fruit contains red seeds, which have been used since pre-Columbian times as a natural dye. Nowadays, it's also used in the cosmetics, textile and food industries.

a tribe, she thought they were joking. It seemed crazy that the man who had left her with an aunt in Lima when she was nine – the neighbourhood's star midfielder, the dancer who loved the Bee Gees and John Travolta, the mixed-race city dweller who never left the house without his shirt ironed and his shoes polished – now wore a tunic, a feather headdress and sandals, and lived in a hut in the middle of the rainforest.

Edwin Chota's sisters were equally shocked. They lived in Ancón, an old fishing village on the north coast of Lima.

'We couldn't believe it,' said Sonia Chota, a housewife, as we sat in the living room of her wooden prefab home. 'My brother even started speaking a strange language.'

To this day, his relatives don't understand why Edwin Chota decided to fight for a community that he wasn't born into. They say that the sudden death of his mother, when he was ten, made him start worrying about other people. From a family with lots of children but very little money, the future Asháninka leader who would one day face the forest mafias was a shy boy, outstanding at school, who used to lend people his belongings to win them over. His siblings and friends say the same thing: Edwin Chota helped people out as a way of making them like him.

There isn't much information about him as a young man. We know he finished secondary school in Pucallpa, then left the smallholding that belonged to his father – a worker who drilled oil wells for an American company – and became a soldier. He fought as a marine in the war between Peru and Ecuador in the 1980s, and then had a job installing high-voltage cables in Iquitos, known as the capital of the Peruvian rainforest. His romantic relationships never lasted long. While he was in the trenches, he had a girlfriend from the Huitoto indigenous nation. Then he had two children – whom the Chota family don't know – with an older woman, a member of an Israelite sect. Some say that during this period Edwin Chota grew a beard and preached the Bible. Then he separated from her, had his daughter Perla with a woman who later left him, and returned to Pucallpa, the story goes, to start afresh.

Elva Risafol, who became his partner when he returned to the city – with whom he had a son called Edwin, now a narcotics police officer – remembers a friend introducing him at a tropical-themed party: he was a skinny thirty-year-old with a mop of straight hair, wearing a sky-blue shirt, jeans and dress shoes. With solemn courtesy, Edwin asked her to dance to 'Sopa de Caracol', and made her laugh with his moves, which Elva liked. That night they talked for hours, and over several beers he told her that he was an electrician, that his ex had left him, that he'd fought in the False Paquisha War, and that he wanted to go back to the rainforest one day and do something for the vulnerable communities there.[2]

'Edwin built his castles in the sky, and you can't live on dreams,' says Risafol, who left him after five years, in 1997. 'I was more practical. I used to tease him and say he'd be happier living with an indigenous woman. I think he took it on board.'

After the break-up, Edwin Chota disappeared from the neighbourhood. Early one morning four years later, Edgar Chota heard a knocking at the door of his house-cum-welding-workshop-cum-food stall in Pucallpa. It was Edwin, his older brother, there for a visit.

'I was so happy to see him,' he recalls. 'We all thought he was dead.'

There is no record of what he did in those four years. People say that towards the end of the 1990s Edwin Chota turned up alone in the Alto Tamaya rainforest. They say he went with some friends to work as a farmhand or a logger or a peccary-leather salesman. They say he went to forget his failures, and stayed because he fell in love with a local woman. What we know for sure is that when

2 The 'False Paquisha War' is the name given to the armed conflict between Peru and Ecuador, which began in January 1981 over the control of some border posts. This short war ended in February of the same year, but it was only in 1998, with the signing of the Brasilia Presidential Act, that the border dispute – begun in 1941 – was finally resolved.

Edwin Chota first set foot in that territory, the Saweto community – named after a green parrot like a macaw, but with a shorter tail – already existed. Or at least the foundations of it did.

The Asháninka came to the Brazilian border from Peru's central rainforest at the beginning of the twentieth century. The rubber boom was in full swing: Europe and the United States were buying up the latex that came from the trees by the tonne, and using it to manufacture car tyres. The indigenous people of the Amazon already knew about rubber: they had always used the sap of the cauchuc – 'crying tree', in the Omagua language – to make balls and basic syringes for injecting narcotics and purgatives. But when the rubber magnates arrived in the rainforest, whole communities were enslaved to extract that raw material which was modernising what would later be known as the First World.

While the rubber barons were transforming Iquitos into an outpost of European extravagance – decking out their homes in hand-painted Italian tiles, installing an opera house and even commissioning an iron mansion designed by the French engineer Gustave Eiffel – just a few kilometres away, with miners' lamps for torches, indigenous men were hacking paths through the jungle with machetes, toiling from dawn to dusk, hunting for rubber trees. On returning to their camps, starving and feverish, they spent hours bent over fires, breathing in smoke that made them feel sick, cooking the rubber on grills until it coagulated. It took weeks to produce a ball large enough to sell. The Saweto Asháninka say their ancestors were swindled time and again over the wages, which were paid in cheap liquor that kept their wits dulled, and that the women were used as servants or made to work on the smallholdings for no pay. Hundreds of native people died of starvation, dysentery, and other diseases.

In 1910, the horrors inflicted on the indigenous people became so notorious that the British government launched an investigation into the camps on the banks of the Putumayo river, near the Colombian border. The Peruvian Amazon Company, one of the most profitable rubber companies of that period, had committed genocide as they attempted to repress and enslave the communities: they had castrated and decapitated indigenous people, doused them with petrol and set them on fire, crucified them upside down, beat them, mutilated them, starved them to death, drowned them and turned them into dog food. The company's henchmen had raped women and smashed children's heads open. All this was described by Roger Casement, the British consul leading the investigation. He estimated that some 30,000 indigenous people died at the hands of the company, which was known as 'the devil's paradise'.[3]

The Saweto Asháninka are likely to be descendants of the native people who came to the Brazilian border during the early twentieth-century rubber boom, along with their old masters. When the rubber ran out, their masters switched to trafficking the skins of exotic animals. When the skins ran out, they moved on to wood. The materials they were pillaging may have changed, but the system that enslaved the indigenous people remained the same.

The Asháninka leaders claim that what happened decades ago is still taking place today: the bosses 'hook' the locals by giving them things – clothes, shotguns, medicines, motors for their boats, radios, food supplies – in exchange for hundreds of tree trunks. Since most of them can't read or write, the bosses lie to them about the quantities and prices, and they end up in debt, forced to chop more wood to pay for the products they have already

3 At the end of the nineteenth century, during the Victorian era, it was widely believed that Amazonian societies were at an inferior stage of evolutionary development, and that they were quite possibly a 'missing link' in the chain between ape and man. In *The Lost City of Z* (2009), David Grann, a *New Yorker* journalist, writes that Richard Burton, a co-founder of the Anthropological Society of London, considered indigenous people a 'subspecies'. Francis Galton, in his theory of eugenics – which counted John Maynard Keynes and Winston Churchill among its followers – maintained that human intelligence is hereditary and unchanging, and that the indigenous peoples of the New World were 'mentally children'.

received. When the loggers turn up, the animals flee the noise of the chainsaws. The Asháninka have to spend more days walking through the wilderness to hunt for food, and sometimes they don't catch anything. The ground is rendered useless for sowing seeds by the logs they have to drag along the ground and the tractors rolling through the forest. The loggers infect the indigenous people with diseases they've never had before. There have been periods when dozens of natives died from a common cold.

More than fifty years later, a new terrorist threat opened another bloody chapter. The Maoist militant group Shining Path arrived in the jungle in the mid-1980s with the aim of gaining control of the whole central rainforest, after clashing with government soldiers in Ayacucho, in the mountains in the south of the country. The terrorists looted farms and set fire to medical clinics and municipal offices. They built forced labour camps deep in the rainforest, where hundreds of Asháninka were held captive for months. They made them work the land, cook for the terrorist leaders, abandon their language and speak Quechua or Spanish. They stabbed or hanged the rebels in front of their families. They raped the women. They kidnapped the children to indoctrinate them and turn them into fighters.

The Asháninka were the Amazonian nation that suffered the most from the war between the army and Shining Path, according to the final Truth and Reconciliation Commission report. More than thirty communities disappeared, some 10,000 indigenous people were displaced, 5,000 were kidnapped and 6,000 were killed – around ten per cent of the total recorded deaths. However, according to the anthropologist Óscar Espinoza, who wrote the section of the report which covered the Asháninka massacre, these statistics don't tell the whole story. When the research was carried out, he recalls, they had no budget and no boats available for visiting all the Amazonian communities. The page count was cut, and details, stories and case studies were removed. The victims' families didn't want to talk.

'An Asháninka mother can't say the name of her dead child. She thinks that, if she does, she'll stop their spirit getting to heaven,' Espinoza tells me one morning, in his office at the Pontifical Catholic University of Peru. 'The Asháninka don't like to speak of their dead.'

Unlike other peoples, who conquer territories, the Asháninka are defensive warriors: as children, they learn to dodge arrows before they learn to fire them. But when they're under attack, when their land is invaded, they have a reputation for being the fiercest fighters – the best with a bow and arrow – of the fifty-one Amazonian nations in Peru.[4]

4 The Saweto Asháninka, known as 'Asháninka of the Gran Pajonal', are also recognised as Ashéninka. They form part of the Asháninka ethnic

By the time Edwin Chota came to Saweto in 1999, Shining Path had been defeated in the central rainforest by government soldiers and the 'Asháninka army': a battalion of indigenous warriors armed with shotguns and bows and arrows, which launched surprise attacks on the Shining Path camps. Around the time of his arrival, a group of Asháninka families from Saweto, which is near the Brazilian border, had also decided to put a stop to the loggers exploiting them, and to seek both state recognition as a community and a title for their land. This, they thought, was the path to freedom.

At first, the timber bosses supported their pursuit of a land title: they thought they could go on chopping down trees and exploiting the Asháninka, even after the land was legally recognised as Asháninka property. But when they saw the legal process moving forwards and Saweto becoming increasingly organised under the leadership of Edwin Chota, they realised that the titling was a threat to their interests. And they weren't going to allow it.

Diana Ríos doesn't remember all the details, but she does remember that she was nine when she met Edwin Chota.

group because they have a shared history and language (with some variations) and because they have traditionally been located in the same region: Peru's central rainforest. As of 2017, the Ashéninka language is in the process of gaining state recognition as a native language.

She recalls seeing him arrive in Saweto alone, extremely thin, carrying his rucksack. He moved into a wooden hut next to her mother, Ergilia Rengifo, the woman who, twelve years later, would be the last person to see him alive.

Back then, the community was in the process of gaining state recognition. They had decided, for the first time, to make the most of their forest and build something really valuable: a bilingual school for their children. And since this newcomer, Edwin Chota, could read and write, he quickly won over the other Asháninka with his willingness to help. They called him Mathari ('Skinny').

One day in 2002, the thirty families of Saweto called a meeting to choose the new community chief. When it came to the vote, most people raised their hand for Chota. They gave him a parcel of land so that he could set up a smallholding. He had been accepted as one of them.

'We used to live separate lives, but Edwin always said we should be more united so people don't trick us,' recalls Diana Ríos, a robust woman in her twenties with a round face and almond-shaped eyes. She's the daughter of one of the three other leaders murdered at the same time as Chota. 'He taught us to read and write; he took me to training sessions for indigenous women. Now I know my rights. He wasn't like other people. He was cheerful, talkative, affectionate like a man. That's why I fell in love with him.'

There are no Asháninka marriage rites. Having children,

for them, means the same as getting married. So we could say that Diana Ríos married Edwin Chota when she was fifteen years old. The couple had a son they called Kitoniro, who grew to be as bright and obstinate as his father. In keeping with their culture's set gender roles, Ríos looked after the child and did the cooking and housework. Chota worked on the smallholding, hunted and brought home meat for the family, and went away for weeks on end to deal with the authorities.

Diana Ríos usually went with Chota to lodge complaints at the regional government offices in Ucayali, several days away by boat. Dressed in traditional brown cushma tunics, with red lines painted on their faces, they would wait outside the door for two, even three hours. Sometimes the authorities refused to see them. Since they didn't have enough money to buy food in the city, the vendors at the port used to give them plantain or fish for free.

In an attempt to defend the forest from illegal loggers, Edwin Chota presented more than a hundred letters to different Peruvian state institutions, demanding the titling of his community: 800 square kilometres of rainforest – almost a quarter of the size of Lima – with rivers running through it that reach all the way to the Brazilian border. But the government refused: it had already assigned eighty per cent of that territory to two Peruvian logging companies. In 2002, a year before Saweto was legally recognised as a community, a civil servant at a desk in Lima had given that land away for the next twenty years without stopping to check who lived there. The area granted to those companies as concessions and the territory of Saweto overlapped like a pair of hands.

For Saweto to receive the property title, the government would need to revoke or relocate those logging concessions. Until that happened, the Asháninka would have no legal right to stop people looting the forest where they lived. They weren't the only ones with that problem. To this day, more than 600 indigenous communities – half the total number in the Peruvian rainforest – are not the legal owners of their land. A study by the World Resources Institute, looking at fifteen countries across Asia, Africa and Latin America, shows that the process of legalising an indigenous territory is extremely complicated, costly and slow, and, in several cases, obliges the families to leave their land or to lose their rights to the water, medicinal plants or foodstuffs it contains. While communities have to face processes that can last more than thirty years, companies seeking concessions in the same areas usually obtain them in just thirty days, and in five years at the most. Indigenous people and rural communities occupy more than half the land on the planet, but they legally own just ten per cent of it. In Peru, gangsters take advantage of this: they tell indigenous communities they will cover the costs of obtaining titles – around $10,000, not including bribes to civil servants – in exchange for permission to cut down their trees.

When Edwin Chota arrived in Saweto, several families were working with the illegal loggers. Communities can live off hunting, fishing and harvests if their forests are intact, but even so, they need things like clothes, soap and medicine, and for many people cutting down trees – or accepting money in exchange for letting people in to do it – is the only way of obtaining them. Chota tried to persuade the Asháninka not to commit these acts of destruction.

'He was direct and he pointed out the corrupt Asháninka chiefs. That's why some people said bad things about him. They said he was going back to Lima, eating in fancy places,' recalls Diana Ríos, who, though she never believed these rumours, decided to separate from the leader after four years because of his long absences. He later began a relationship with another Asháninka woman, Julia Pérez, with whom he had a son, Tsonkiri.

This is how Edwin Chota spent twelve years of his life. His priority was demarcating the territory and defining its limits. This meant that, as well as making accusations and complaints to the state, he ensured that Saweto had something as basic as a map. Faced with companies and governments used to denying or downplaying the depredation, Chota thought the Asháninka should use the language of cartography – co-ordinates, boundary markers, aerial photographs – as a weapon to defend what they considered theirs.

Peru, the cliché goes, is an Andean country. 'The land of the Inca', people call it, inside and outside its borders. In terms of geographical area, however, it's an Amazonian country first and foremost. After Brazil, Peru has the greatest area of rainforest in Latin America: almost seventy per cent of its surface is covered by jungle. But if someone looked at a map of concessions to extraction companies, they would notice that for the past half-century the Peruvian Amazon has been divided into dozens of rectangles called 'lots', which are handed over to logging, oil and mining companies to be explored and, ultimately, exploited.

With only this map to go by, one might assume that the rainforest contains nothing but trees, rivers and animals. In other words: no people, no communities, no cultures. The cartographer Brian Harley explains that these 'empty spaces' on a map are really 'silences': information the map deliberately hides. A map is not an innocent drawing: it contains a political message.

David Salisbury, a geography professor at the University of Richmond in the United States, knew Edwin Chota and helped him to publicise his struggle outside Peru. During the years he lived in the rainforest, Salisbury, a tall, slim man with blond hair and a kindly voice, advised Asháninka communities on how to use maps to identify the deforested zones threatening their land and culture. Saweto was one of the communities he worked with.

'The official maps don't show the reality of the Amazon,' Salisbury explained to me over Skype. 'The native communities don't appear on the official cartography. And the populations that don't appear on those maps are the ones that suffer most from illegal logging and rights violations. Titling and creating a map of Saweto protected the community, along with their forest and everything in it. The loggers no longer had free rein. Chota changed the status quo. That's why they wanted him dead.'

The history of nations shows that drawing a line across a map can shape the course of millions of lives. A map is an instrument of power. And nowadays, map experts in Peru tend to work in state institutions which give these tools to people with economic and political influence. Hardly anyone knows who they are, but they produce detailed information on the country's rivers, mountains and forests. Six hundred years ago, nautical charts turned Spain, Portugal and England into empires. Today, the same kind of knowledge is often used to further the interests of powerful business conglomerates.

In Peru, these maps are usually drawn up by specialist

bodies, such as the National Aerophotographic Service and the National Geographic Institute. They are used by various state offices, such as the Ministry of Agriculture and the Intelligence Service, but also by mining, logging and oil companies that have permission from the government to exploit natural resources. These companies usually pay thousands of dollars for detailed maps of the mountain and rainforest areas that interest them, maps which, as a rule, remain in these companies' possession for ten years.

'Can you imagine what native communities could do with that information? They could produce development plans, guard their territory better,' said Wendy Pineda, a geographical engineer from Rainforest Foundation US, an NGO that provides legal advice to the Saweto widows on their husbands' murder case. 'When you ask why those maps aren't shared with the indigenous people, the state tells you: "They'll have access to that data within a few years." But that almost never happens. And if it does, it's too late, because the communities' land is already being exploited. The information goes to the highest bidder first.'

Seventy per cent of the Peruvian rainforest is shared out between these extraction companies. While on some concession maps the companies are shown as polygons – large areas of land – the native communities are represented by dots, like small, scattered archipelagos.

'But the communities are polygons too!' said Pineda, a woman from Lima with long hair, dark skin and attentive eyes, who after Edwin Chota's death trained Asháninka communities in Ucayali to develop their own maps using drones and GPS devices. 'The state draws them as dots so that everything outside them is considered free to be exploited.'

It doesn't matter if a population has been living on the same land for generations. According to Professor Salisbury and Pineda the engineer, the historical logic of many governments is simple and perverse: if something's not on the map, it doesn't exist.

The Asháninka avoid conflict. If one of them gets angry with a neighbour, that person usually goes off into the woodland by themselves to calm down and then comes back to talk it over. For an Asháninka – which in their language means 'our brothers' – there is nothing worse than hating or killing a member of the family.

The Asháninka share food. If one goes to another's house, he or she is served a drink called 'masato' – made from yucca fermented with saliva – and something to eat, without having to ask. Plantain, maize, cacao, sweet potato and beans make up eighty per cent of their diet, along with other foodstuffs they grow on their smallholdings. Where they live, no one owns the land or the hunting and fishing sites. The idea of individual private property is alien to them.

The Asháninka are all each other's uncles, aunts, cousins, nieces and nephews. They're all family. It doesn't matter if they belong to another community or if they don't share the same surname. There are no lineages or social classes. Their Western surnames – Arévalo, Pérez, Ríos – come from the old owners of the land where they worked, and from missionaries who wanted their names to be easy to recognise. In public registries, the staff used to change their names and surnames for convenience.

The Asháninka communities have chiefs. The chief is usually a man who leads the rest by dint of his strong character and powers of persuasion.

'You don't need to be an Asháninka to be a chief, you just need to have love for us, for our culture,' says Ergilia Rengifo, Chota's former mother-in-law and neighbour. 'One man's the same as another.'

Edwin Chota the electrician didn't speak Asháninka fluently, but he managed to organise his community in such a way that it had far more than the food packages from social programmes that went to the neighbouring hamlet. In his first years as leader, Saweto acquired electricity through solar panels, a two-channel radio to communicate with the city, a raised tank for water and a preschool. The community members received ID papers for the first time:

now they existed as citizens. Before he died, Chota oversaw the construction of a building for the primary school, which until then had operated from his house. He achieved all this thanks to his persistence in dealing with the municipality and the regional government, support from various organisations, and the alliance he forged with the Asháninka of the Apiwtxa community, in the Brazilian state of Acre, to defend the forest on both sides of the border. Chota also wanted what the Brazilian indigenous people had: a hatchery for turtle eggs and another for fish, a garden of flowers for export, and replanted forests. Apiwtxa, for him, was an example of 'development'.

But he didn't rely only on his charisma for building alliances, or on his determination when making demands. The environmental anthropologist Mario Osorio, who wrote his master's thesis on Saweto at the University of Kent, recalls that a few days before going out to file paperwork, Chota would fast and take ayahuasca, 'the vine of the spirits'. He said that this hallucinogenic plant, sacred to Amazonian peoples, helped him connect with the rainforest.

'For Edwin, protecting the forests was a spiritual struggle,' recalls the anthropologist Osorio, who became friends with Chota during the months he lived in his hut. Osorio taught him to use Microsoft Word and send emails. Chota taught him the customs of his people.

The Asháninka have a profound belief in the power of evil. From them, Edwin Chota learnt that there were invisible enemies in the world and that he had to defeat them as well. The elders call them 'kamári': demons. Spirits that hide in the forest, in the caves. Malevolent beings that grind people's bones, that suck out their eyes. They can kill a newborn baby or the strongest warrior. They can possess a person, Asháninka or not, and make them murder their own brother without a second's thought. Kamári are the essence of evil, and the illegal loggers, like the terrorists before them, are some of their more recent incarnations.

Perhaps because he was all too aware of the risk, Chota spoke very little about his other family, the one he left in the city. For the twelve years his struggle lasted, only those closest to him – the other Asháninka leaders, his wife – knew he'd once had another life. Chota had split his reality in two: his children Perla and Edwin were in the city, and his sons Kitoniro ('Scorpion') and Tsonkiri ('Hummingbird') were in the community. It was better that way. The illegal loggers were on his tail. He didn't want to put his relatives in danger.

'But sometimes he also said to us: "What are you doing, suffering here? In the city, if you don't buy things, you don't eat. But in the forest you can find everything: animals, yucca, fish. There you'd have everything you need",' Edwin's father remembers. 'He wanted to take us with him so that we could be Asháninka too. He didn't like it if you said anything bad about them.'

One night Edwin Chota met his siblings in Pucallpa to go to a party and dance cumbia. He showed up with two Asháninka women, who were barefoot and wearing cushmas. His siblings were annoyed.

'Edwin had a go at us, he told us we're all the same, that we should accept our race, that we're indigenous too,' his brother Edgar recalls. 'He loved that culture.'

Chota used to say that he'd had an Asháninka teacher at secondary school who taught him not to be ashamed of his roots. He also swore that one of his grandmothers had been born in an Amazonian community in Iquitos, but her relatives denied it. What made him angriest was realising that people – politicians, businesspeople, citizens, his own family – believed, in their heart of hearts, that being indigenous meant being savage, poor and inferior.

Perla Chota learnt how much being Asháninka mattered to her father when she saw him again in Pucallpa when she was eighteen. He was dressed as an indigenous leader. 'My first reaction was to ignore him,' recalls Perla – now a slim 26-year-old with dyed-brown hair and lively dark eyes, and the mother of three girls. She was a waitress in a barbecue chicken restaurant at the time. When they met at a relative's house, Edwin Chota apologised 'for being a bad father' and leaving her with an aunt when she was little. He wanted her to understand that he'd left 'to fight for something important'. Perla remembers that they spoke for hours, crying and hugging, and then went out for dinner. The next day, Chota took her to an Asháninka village on the other side of the Ucayali river, where he used to stay when he had business in Pucallpa. There, he introduced her to her little brothers.

'Walk with me,' she remembers her father saying.

Perla didn't really understand what he meant, but she was happy they were together again. However, the reconciliation didn't last. Days later, while Chota was having lunch with some foreigners, he saw his daughter walking down the street and called her over so he could introduce her. Perla says she wasn't paying attention, didn't hear him and carried on walking. When they met again a few hours later, her father reproached her: 'You're ashamed of me because I'm an Asháninka.' They yelled at each other. They argued. She gave back the multicoloured seed bracelet he'd given her and left without saying goodbye. Eight years later, on a grey avenue in Lima, while passengers were boarding the bus on the Villasol–Santa Anita line where she worked as a conductor, her mobile rang. Someone was calling to say that her father had been in the news.

'He never cared about me, but I feel good knowing the things he did,' Perla Chota told me in a wavering voice

when I met her. '"Your father's going to be a great man,"
he told me. He had to die before that could come true.'

Since the late 1990s, Edwin Chota and the Saweto
Asháninka had looked on, powerless, as groups of loggers
armed with machetes and shotguns stole their trees. They
transported them from the headwaters of the Alto
Tamaya and Putaya rivers, sailing for more than a week, to
the sawmills in Pucallpa. When Chota reported them, the
authorities told him the inspectors would only investigate
if he paid for the boat, food and fuel they would need to
reach his community's area of the rainforest.

'Who will defend us? Who will defend our forest?'
Chota demanded in an interview with some *New York
Times* journalists, who had gone to a sawmill to investigate
illegal logging. 'We're threatened with death. Death is
welcome. There's no law. There's no money to investigate.
There's only money to destroy.'

There was one man who met him and tried to ensure
justice was done. One morning in April 2013, Edwin
Chota showed up in the office of Francisco Berrospi,
a public prosecutor, to report that more than 800
shihuahuaco and cedar logs had been illegally extracted
from his community and were at a sawmill in the port of
Pucallpa. Berrospi – a lawyer born in Huánuco, a region of
snowfalls, warm valleys and cloud forests – recalls that

when he met the Asháninka leader, he understood that his work as a civil servant went beyond gathering evidence he could use against the illegal loggers before a judge.

'Edwin had a very strong connection to the forest,' I was told by the former prosecutor, a man with tortoise-shell glasses, a dark suit and a prominent chin, the afternoon we met in a cafe in central Lima. 'And he knew how to get it across.'

That morning in 2013, Berrospi – who had been in his post as the environmental prosecutor of Ucayali, the region with the most sawmills in Peru, for just five months – decided to listen to Chota. He got up from his desk, hung his prosecutor's insignia round his neck, and together they set out for the port.

'Touch it,' Chota told him at the sawmill, laying his hand on an enormous log of shihuahuaco, a species of tree that can live for up to 700 years and is now in danger of disappearing. 'Doesn't it feel like a relative has died?'

In the afternoon, when he returned to the prosecutor's office after all that wood had been seized, the Asháninka leader found a furious man awaiting him. It was Hugo Soria, the professed owner of the confiscated logs. 'Someone from Saweto is going to die,' the logger taunted him in front of another prosecutor, who later recorded the threat in writing, 'and I'm going to report you as a narco-trafficker.'

After that, various rumours about Chota began to spread. That he came from Vraem, a valley in the central rainforest threatened by narco-terrorists. That he had crops of coca leaves in Saweto and maceration pits for the paste. That he smuggled drugs into Brazil and was wanted by the federal police there. That he bought houses in Pucallpa with dirty money. That he poisoned the river to kill his adversaries' cattle. That he was exploiting the Asháninka. That he was an illegal logger himself. That Edwin Chota Valera wasn't his real name, and he'd changed it to evade the law. He was accused of all these things in the criminal prosecutor's office in Ucayali by a representative of ECOFUSAC, one of the concessions on Saweto's land, as revenge for his accusations. The prosecutor's office and the narcotics police investigated Chota for a year. They found nothing. The case was closed in June 2014, but the death threats and slander continued. Edwin Chota had got under the mafias' skin.

Timber trafficking would be the forestry equivalent of drug trafficking, except for one detail: as an activity, chopping down trees is not forbidden, unlike producing and trafficking cocaine. All you need to make it lawful is documents certifying that the wood has legal origins. Once the tree has fallen, you simply have to show that it's from an authorised source. The problem is that these processes are deeply susceptible to corruption.

In its 2012 report *The Laundering Machine*, the Environmental Investigation Agency (EIA), which specialises in ecological crimes, sets out how the system works. Under Peruvian forestry law, each logging company must submit an annual inventory of all the trees on the relevant parcel of its concession that it plans to fell during that year. But often, these lists include trees growing on adjacent land, and the companies receive approval to sell hundreds of cubic metres of wood that doesn't belong to them. Since nobody checks up on them in the forest, the process is simple: they declare that they're chopping down certified species of wood, but in their lorries they transport another species that's in danger of extinction. They say they are chopping down wood in a permitted area of the forest, but really they do it in a native community. They cut down 700 trees and only declare half. In Peru there are eight million hectares of forest concessions for extraction: equivalent to almost seven million football pitches put together. An article in *Scientific Reports* asserts that more than sixty per cent of the concessions granted by the Peruvian state are a front for laundering wood.[5]

---

5 In its 2018 report, *Moment of Truth*, the EIA states that despite advances in the struggle against the illegal felling, laundering and international trafficking of Peruvian timber, systemic corruption is still rife. The logging industry, its main regulating authority (the National Forest and Wildlife Service) and other state bodies have denied or downplayed the problem. They have attempted to weaken the

'Logging happens everywhere except where it's legally supposed to,' says Julia Urrunaga, director of Peru programmes at the EIA. 'To steal those trees you have to violate the rights of a lot of people. In the capital, a long way from the forest, no one cares about that.'

Wood laundering happens every day, with the authorities' permission. The papers used to launder wood are official permits full of false information, and easy to buy on the black market. The only kinds of wood traceable under current legal requirements in Peru are those in danger of extinction – such as cedar and mahogany, used to make top-of-the-range furniture in the United States – thanks to the information required to obtain export permits. But when it comes to other valuable species – like the teak bought by China, the main consumer of illegal Peruvian wood, to make parquet floors – there's no way of tracing them. Although the exporters have to provide origin information for all species of wood, in practice it's not a legal requirement for exportation, and therefore many businesses don't do it. When those trees reach customs sawn into boards, tracing their origin is like following ant footprints.

'We can't check if all the wood shipments are legal

institutions that enforce the regulations. They have cut back on data collection and changed the export requirements, making it almost impossible to trace timber and verify its legal origin.

because we don't have the resources,' the engineer Marcial Pezo admitted when I visited his office on the outskirts of Pucallpa. 'If the wood has official papers, it goes through. I'm not psychic.'

Outside the Forestry and Wildlife Directorate, the institution led by Pezo which is in charge of granting logging licences, there are hundreds of confiscated logs – copaiba, catahua, moena, cashimo, ishpingo, capirona and other trees with ancestral names – rotting from the damp and rain. Some of that wood is returned to the alleged owners when they show up with their 'papers in order' to take it away. In Pezo's office – where Chota (unsuccessfully) tried to process the titling of Saweto – there's a pair of armchairs made from confiscated cedar.

By 2014, the year Edwin Chota was murdered, the president of the Ucayali region, Jorge Velázquez, had been reported more than a hundred times for misappropriation of funds. The vice president, a logging executive, had been fined by the state for laundering illegal wood. The forestry inspectors reported for signing fraudulent permits remained in their posts. The fact that most reports of illegal logging – nine out of every ten that reach the prosecutor's office – go nowhere is merely a sign that the corrupt system is working. Eighty per cent of the wood exported by Peru has illegal origins, according to reports from the World Bank. In 2014, Interpol and the World Customs

Organisation carried out an operation against illegal logging in the country, and seized enough logs in just three months to fill almost 700 removal lorries. During the operation, timber exports fell by half. Every year, Peru loses some $250m in taxes avoided by illegal loggers. This is more than the legal forestry industry makes in the same time period.

Laundering wood is a profitable business. Aside from transport, the costs are low, and there's no need to worry about paying decent salaries or following environmentally friendly practices. Felling a large tree in the Peruvian rainforest produces some three cubic metres of export-quality wood. The gangsters rub their hands with glee: one cubic metre of mahogany, $1,700. One of cedar, $1,000. And when that wood hits the market in the United States, those prices triple. Thirty per cent of the wood sold worldwide is illegal. It's a business whose turnover – according to the United Nations Environment Programme – is as much as $152,000 million a year: double what Apple, Google and Facebook made in 2017 combined. And it's less risky than the stock market: a study conducted in Brazil, the Philippines, Indonesia and Mexico found that the probability of an illegal logging crime being punished is 0.082 per cent. The situation is worst in countries that are inefficiently governed, corrupt or suffer from political violence.

Illegal logging doesn't, at first glance, have the criminal stamp of drug trafficking. Cocaine is an addictive substance, whereas wood from the Amazon is used to make houses, tables, chairs and other kinds of furniture. Not many people realise that in the Alto Tamaya rainforest, as in other areas of the Peruvian jungle, indigenous workers are chopping down wood in conditions close to slavery; that cooks in logging camps are raped by the loggers; that indigenous leaders and civil servants are threatened and killed for not accepting bribes. The United Nations sees timber trafficking as similar to the 'blood diamonds' that have financed wars and large-scale human rights violations in Africa. Nevertheless, the authorities in Pucallpa, a city built on the edge of the Amazon rainforest, go on receiving reports that nobody looks into. No logger has ever been sent to prison for felling or trafficking trees in Peru.

'Illegal things become legal here. It's all done with tricks and bribes.'

Adjusting the knot in his blue tie every now and then, the former prosecutor Francisco Berrospi tells me that during 2013 he had to travel to remote areas of the rainforest to pursue most of his investigations, but his office had no boats or helicopters he could use to reach inaccessible logging fields. When he seized trucks, chainsaws and trees, the judges generally forced him to return them. Bribes were so common that one anti-corruption prosecutor encouraged him to take the $5,000 he was being offered to call off an investigation. 'Listen,' he remembers his colleague saying, 'in a year here you can make enough cash to build yourself a house, buy a car. It's better that way.' Once, Berrospi seized seventy logs. A judge quickly ordered him to return them to the logger.

'You know what she told me?' the prosecutor asks, smiling sardonically. '"How can I send someone to prison for seventy logs if there are millions of trees in the rainforest?"'

Berrospi had become a nuisance, a piece that didn't fit. Sometimes people phoned him up at night to threaten him. 'You're going to die, you dog. What do you think you are? A hero?' And then, in August 2013, two days after seizing a light aircraft from the Peruvian air force carrying a box of twenty-four kilograms of unauthorised mahogany seeds – in Europe, a kilo is worth $6,000 – the prosecutor was removed from his post for 'internal reasons'. Soon after that, more than 800 logs from the Pucallpa sawmill, seized with Edwin Chota's help, were returned to Hugo Soria, the furious logger. Another case closed.

'I was frustrated, I was shouting with rage,' Berrospi admitted, frowning, his voice subdued. 'But Chota wasn't like that. He complained but then he calmed down, shook his head and asked himself why they weren't investigating. He said I was out of touch with nature, and that was why I got so mad. That I should walk barefoot to connect with the earth. Tolstoy said that when men look at the forest they only see firewood. Edwin told me something similar. That's why I always remember when he made me touch that log in the sawmill. I felt really sad, like when you're at a funeral.'

The last time Edwin Chota was in Lima was for the Independence Day celebrations in July 2014. His complaints were being ignored in Pucallpa, so he visited various central government institutions to present his demands one more time: he went to Congress, he met with representatives of the Presidency of the Council of Ministers, he asked for help from the Office of the Human Rights Ombudsman, he alerted the forestry authorities. 'From dawn till dusk, sometimes on no food, Edwin waited in those offices for an answer,' says Margoth Quispe, previously the human rights ombudsman in Ucayali and Chota's legal adviser, who is speaking to me from Rome. Of all the institutions, only the inspectors from the Agency for the Supervision of Forestry Resources and Wildlife – responsible for penalising illegal logging – agreed to visit Saweto soon.

Two days before he was killed, the inspectors arrived in the community. Chota joined them on the tour of the forest. In their report – published after the four Asháninka leaders' deaths – the experts concluded that the two concessions on Saweto territory, ECOFUSAC and Ramiro Edwin Barrios Galván, were chopping down unauthorised species, with no work plan and without paying tax. It was the first time the authorities had come to verify what Chota had been reporting for more than a decade.

The friends who were murdered along with him told Chota's wife that he was feeling weak during the inspection, and didn't eat anything. He almost died out there. The loggers, who had set up their illegal camps in the depths of the forest, threatened him. 'We're coming in whether you like it or not,' one crowed, stroking his shotgun. 'We'll see who wins: the community or us.'

José Borgo, a conservation expert and the co-ordinator of ProPurús, an NGO that supports Saweto's defence of its land, was good friends with Edwin Chota. He's a dark-skinned man in his sixties with grey hair and a considerable paunch. One baking-hot afternoon, he met me in his bar, Don José, a bustling joint on the Pucallpa boardwalk where port workers toast each other with beer as cumbias and boleros by Lucho Barrios blast out at full volume.

Borgo met Chota in 2002, when he was beginning his fight to gain a property title for his community. The leader would usually come and sit in a corner of his bar when he travelled to the city by boat to file papers. When he heard about the murder, Borgo spent days putting together a folder of more than 200 pages: all the letters, proposals, applications and complaints that Edwin Chota had pre-sented during the course of ten years, all ignored. Borgo also wrote five names into his little orange notebook. It was his list of suspects.

'You know what I find most outrageous?' Borgo asked me. He was sitting in a rocking chair, sweaty and shirtless, voice shaking with rage after reading the list. 'Not one of the complaints Edwin made against these sons of bitches went anywhere. Not one.'

Borgo passed the information on to the widows' lawyer. However, during the first year of the investigation, only two of the loggers suspected of the crime were arrested. The police froze the case for several months, along with the search for the last of the bodies, due to lack of funds.

That sweltering afternoon on the boardwalk, perhaps convinced of the inevitable impunity, Borgo told me he had his rucksack packed. He was ready to get on a boat and travel upriver to Saweto, where he would investigate his friend's death for himself.

In one of the few interviews with Edwin Chota you can find on YouTube, from April 2013, the Asháninka leader is sitting on the ground in his hiding place. You can see his seed bracelet and missing tooth, and his eyes look tired. He says: 'I'm going to take the lead for my community. Maybe someone has to die before they'll listen to us.'

It wasn't the first time he had warned of this. In 2005, six years after he first set foot in Saweto, Chota asked the Peruvian government for protection for him and the families in his community, because the illegal loggers were threatening to kill them. There was no response. One year later, he reported a logger who was intimidating the Asháninka leaders. The court took no notice. The cycle went on for years: Edward Chota reporting the illegal loggers and them responding with death threats. The government did nothing. In 2012, he once again reported the deforestation of his community's land to the Pucallpa environmental prosecutor, but the case was closed. The next year, the Asháninka leader located every illegal camp using a GPS device, and photographed the loggers with their chainsaws as they felled enormous trees more than a hundred years old in the space of half an hour. Chota showed the evidence to the police, along with the first names and surnames of the loggers. That case was closed as well. In 2014, five months before he was killed, Edwin Chota spoke out one more time: the same loggers, the same death threats, the same lack of response. The Pucallpa authorities claimed not to have the money to go to Saweto and investigate whether what the Asháninka chief was saying was true.

'I'm looking at a void,' he said to the camera, from the refuge on the border that some Brazilian friends had found him for his protection. 'In Saweto we feel the lack of institutions, of our own government. For them it's like we don't exist.'

To prevent the titling of the forest, the log traffickers tried to get Edwin Chota out of the way: they offered him bribes of up to $10,000, and they accused him of making money from organisations that supported indigenous people. Then they moved on to threats. They stole the motors from the communal boat in Saweto, plundered the crops and animals, shot at the welcome sign outside the community and the Peruvian flag the Asháninka raised each week when they sang the national anthem. At night the loggers walked around the houses, shooting into the air. They spread a rumour that 'someone' from the community was going to die if they keep 'fucking around'. In Saweto everyone knew that 'someone' was Edwin Chota.

After the sudden death of a loved one, we often believe that their last words to us, a certain dream we had or even the song of a bird were signs of what was to come. Days before they learnt of his death, Edwin Chota's siblings say, they were told about it in their sleep. Edgar, a welder, dreamt that a huge vulture landed on the door to his house and he had to scare it off with a stick. Gilma, a shopkeeper, dreamt she was digging a grave with her bare hands. Fernando, a baker, dreamt he was at a party with people laughing uproariously.

'Now I know that meant a funeral,' Fernando said to me, solemn-faced. 'The next day I had a phone call telling me my brother was dead.'

The day before he was shot, Edwin Chota also had a dream: he was in a field in the middle of the rainforest with his mother, grandfather and uncle, all of whom had died years before. 'They were calling him,' says Julia Pérez, his widow, a slim, quiet woman in her thirties with a mistrustful gaze. In the early hours of that morning, with her six-month-pregnant belly, Julia was woken by her husband moaning in his sleep. It was four in the morning. Chota got up, trembling. He was drenched in sweat. He pulled on some old jeans, a long-sleeved white shirt – which he would later swap for a black one – and some wellies. He packed his mosquito net and a change of clothes in his rucksack, sorted out his folder of documents and got ready to go to the Apiwtxa Asháninka community in Acre. There, along with the Brazilian leaders under attack from the same loggers, they would plan how to defend their land.

That morning Edwin Chota behaved strangely. 'He looked ill, he barely said a word,' his widow recalls. He didn't want to eat the breakfast his wife had made him, so she packed the rice, meat and stewed yucca in a bag for the two-day journey to the border. Chota wasn't exactly an affectionate father, but he hugged his children, seven-year-old Kitoniro and two-year-old Tsonkiri, before getting into the peque peque, a motorised canoe. Julia thought her husband was hung-over from the masato he'd drunk the night before at the opening ceremony for a smallholding, as was the Asháninka custom.

Ergilia Rengifo, the wife of Jorge Ríos – the Saweto treasurer murdered along with Edwin Chota – doesn't remember much. She doesn't remember how old she is, or her ID number. One of the few things she retains in her memory is this: the morning the leaders set off for the border, the chicua bird screeched more loudly than usual. For the Asháninka, the chicua is a bird that announces bad news. It's a kind of dwarf sparrowhawk with brown feathers that lives in the rainforest, and when it sings – chicua, chicua! – the Asháninka think something terrible will happen: someone will die by falling in the river, getting bitten by a snake or being cursed by an act of witchcraft.

'You'd better not go,' Ergilia begged them. 'The chicua's getting mad, that's bad luck.'

'It's fine,' her husband tried to reassure her. 'What does the chicua know? Besides, all four of us are going. Just pray to the Lord, that's all.'

Ergilia made them fried boquichico and cacharama fish with stewed yucca for breakfast. 'But by then I couldn't relax,' Ríos's widow recalls. 'Birds don't make mistakes.' After her husband's death, Ergilia said she'd seen Eurico

Mapes, an illegal logger and one of the suspected murderers, going up the river in his peque peque. Mapes was staring straight at the Asháninka leaders, as if counting them.

Minutes before setting off for the border, Edwin and Ergilia discussed the latest threats he'd received.

'I've signed my own death warrant,' Chota said to his neighbour. Then he set off into the forest.

It was ten in the morning on 1 September 2014.

Six hours later, a bullet from a shotgun ended his life.

Three weeks after the Asháninka leaders were murdered in the Peruvian jungle, a white banner with Edwin Chota's face on it was waving in the streets of New York. Almost half a million people from different cities around the world had gathered for the biggest environmental march in history, days before the UN Climate Summit. Journalists, politicians, activists and celebrities – from the former vice president of the United States, Al Gore, and the United Nations Secretary-General, Ban Ki-moon, to Leonardo DiCaprio and Sting – took to the streets to demand their governments take concrete action against the pollution and depredation of the planet. The Peruvian activists held up the banner with Chota's face and signs showing the names of the murdered Asháninka leaders, demanding that the culprits were found. By then, the *Wall Street Journal*, *National Geographic*, the BBC and *El País* had published reports on Chota's murder and his battle to prevent the looting of the forest where he and his family lived. An article in *Folha de São Paulo* said that Chota 'was a Chico Mendes of his time', comparing him to the famous Brazilian rubber tapper and activist murdered at the end of the 1980s for defending the Amazon. The Lima press called Edwin Chota a 'martyr of the rainforest'. For those Peruvians in New York, the Asháninka leader symbolised something more: the risks someone will take to fight for what they believe is right.

But more than 5,000 kilometres from that march, on the other side of the Andes, in the port of Pucallpa where Chota was born and raised, few people knew who he was. 'Chota? I saw something on the news. He's the achaninga who got killed, isn't he?' the shopkeeper Francisco Muñoz said doubtfully. 'He went around with savages, they're not civilised. They used to eat people. Now they attack you. They fire arrows at you,' warned the street photographer Jorge Aliaga. 'I gave him a lift in my boat. He was a good guy,' the fisherman Santiago Luna recalled. 'No one knew him here in Pucallpa. They're the leaders of their communities, they stay around there,' said Richard Romaina, a security guard on the boardwalk. 'He's the man who went around in a tunic, his face all painted,' said Luisa Rivera, a food seller. 'Do you know why they killed him?'

Being an activist who defends a territory can be a

misunderstood and thankless task. These days, it also means accepting you might be killed. Four environmentalists are murdered in the world every week, and the list of victims speaks volumes. In 2001, the indigenous leader Kimy Pernía was murdered by Colombian paramilitaries after opposing the construction of a reservoir. In 2003, Ángel Shingre from Ecuador was kidnapped and shot for taking an oil company to court. In 2009, the indigenous Mexican Mariano Abarca was shot outside the door of his home for protesting against a mining company. In 2011, the Congolese man Frédéric Moloma was beaten to death by police officers during a protest against deforestation. In 2012, the Cambodian activist Chut Wutty was murdered by soldiers for denouncing illegal loggers. That same year, the Filipino leader Jimmy Liguyon was shot dead in front of his wife for opposing a mining project. In 2015, the Honduran woman Berta Cáceres held up the construction of a reservoir in a river that was sacred to the Lenca people, and was shot in her own home. More than a thousand environmentalists worldwide have died in the past twelve years, according to Global Witness. On a planet where resources are scarce, defending a forest or a piece of land has never been a matter for cossetted idealists or tree huggers: in 2011, to frighten people off reporting illegal logging, some hitmen shot a Brazilian couple who were defending a nature reserve. Then they cut off their ears.

Global Witness also tells us that, in 2017, Peru was the seventh most dangerous country in the world and the fourth most dangerous in America – after Brazil, Colombia and Mexico – for environmental activism. In 2008, Julio García Agapito, the lieutenant governor of a town on the Bolivian border, was shot eight times in the local forestry authority office after he stopped a lorry transporting illicit mahogany. The murder went unpunished. In 2013 two hitmen on motorbikes shot and killed Mauro Pío, a long-standing Asháninka leader. For twenty years, Pío had been demanding a title for his land and the expulsion of the forestry company that was invading his community. More than eighty Peruvians were murdered for similar reasons in the first two decades of this century. This figure only includes the cases we know about.

'The greatest danger we feel is that the state, which is supposed to defend us, will betray us,' Ruth Buendía, a renowned Asháninka leader, told me on hearing of Edwin Chota's death. Buendía fought the Brazilian company Odebrecht to prevent the construction of a reservoir on indigenous land. 'The government leaves us at the mercy of criminals.'

Until the last day of his life, Chota was preparing to take Saweto's case to the Inter-American Court of Human Rights. 'As long as we don't have a title, the loggers don't respect native ownership,' the Asháninka leader told Scott

Wallace, a *National Geographic* journalist who travelled to Saweto in 2013 to cover mahogany trafficking. 'They threaten us. They intimidate us. They have the guns.' Because of the threats, Wallace writes, Chota often had to seek refuge with his fellow Asháninka in Brazil, a two-day walk away. It was by the side of that same footpath that his and his friends' bodies would later be found.

Edwin Chota's sisters came across Wallace's article online when, some days after the fact, an uncle told them about the death of their older brother, whom they hadn't seen for ten years. In their desperation, all they could think to do was leave a comment on the magazine's website in the hope of attracting some media attention:

LUZ CHOTA VALERA PERU 9 SEPTEMBER, 1:21 P.M.

We are the sisters of Edwin Chota Valera, we're very sad about what has happened to our brother, our names are Sonia and Luz Chota Valera, we are living in Lima and we feel desperate about my brother, his body is being eaten by animals, we have a phone number ******, we have read your comment but we don't know English, we are humble and simple people but with the same principles as my brother, he spoke out about the danger his life was in and the lives of his Asháninka brothers and sisters but the authorities in my country did nothing, this is all so unfair, we would be grateful if you could help us with justice not only for my brother but also for our people and our nature, I still don't know if you have heard my family's sad news. Thank you very much.

Luz and Sonia Chota – who some time later would move to Santiago de Chile to work in a restaurant – had to borrow money and pawn their television and hi-fi to buy a pair of bus tickets and travel the twenty hours to Pucallpa to identify the body.

Meanwhile, two days after the first news of the murder, the police sub-officer Carlos Napaico was getting into a Mi-17 helicopter to travel to Cusco and deal with some social unrest over the exploitation of a natural gas reserve. But then he had a call from his commander, assigning him to a new mission: he and his seventy colleagues – all 'anti-subversive' police officers – were to fly to the Alto Tamayo rainforest, on the border with Brazil, to find the bodies of 'some Asháninka'.

With no special diving equipment, the police plunged into the pit of brown, stinking water to look for the body. After searching for five days with the help of the Asháninka hunter Jaime Arévalo, sub-officer Napaico found the remains. Since they had no radio to communicate with, they put Edwin Chota's bones in a sack, tied them up tightly and waited in some improvised shelters made from tree branches, eating tins of tuna and soda crackers for two rainy days, until the army helicopter came to collect them. For sub-officer Napaico, twenty-eight years old, the Asháninka leader's body was his 'ticket out': once he and his colleagues found the body, his superiors had told him, they could leave.

When a leader becomes a martyr, people remember him as the embodiment of their own struggles. Now, after his death, Edwin Chota will represent many things for his followers: resistance to illegal logging, the defence of indigenous rights, the lonely battle of someone hoping for a justice that never comes, the strange bravery of a man from the countryside taking on the state. For the four Saweto widows, their husbands' deaths are proof of how far the Asháninka will go to be heard.

'Without a property title I'm worth nothing,' said Ergilia Rengifo, one of the widows, when she went to Lima at the end of 2014 to present her case to the press. 'We look after the water, the forests. We don't look after them only for ourselves, but for the people who live in the city as well. We're not poor. I'm rich, on my land I have everything. The poor ones are the loggers who steal what we have.'

The Saweto women decided to persevere with their

husbands' demands until they managed to get a title for their land. Diana Ríos, Chota's ex-partner and the daughter of one of the other three murdered leaders, travelled to New York to accept the annual prize from the Alexander Soros Foundation – a posthumous recognition of the indigenous leaders as environmental heroes – and a sum of money to fund the projects that Edwin Chota was unable to finish. His death led to the Peruvian government beginning the process of titling Saweto and investing around $300,000 in plans to grow cacao and medicinal plants, and in the replanting of timber-yielding forests.[6] In 2014, President Humala promised a thorough investigation into the murders, but in September 2018, four years after the crime, the investigation was still going on. The four people arrested during the trial – including Eurico Mapes, one of the suspected murderers – were released.

'They've offered us everything, but it's all blah-blah-blah, nothing but words,' Julia Pérez, Chota's widow, told the reporters' cameras. 'We never see the results.' The widows feared the loggers would take revenge when they returned to their community.

Edwin Chota's family couldn't bury his remains until

6   In August 2015, almost a year after the murder of Edwin Chota and his friends, the Saweto community received the property title for around 300 square miles of land. But the community members are not yet satisfied. They continue to demand that their leaders' murderers are caught. They say the illegal loggers are still threatening them.

five months after his murder. More than a hundred people – local representatives, activists, friends – attended the funeral at Pucallpa General Cemetery. The body was cremated. His widow, with the baby in her arms, laid the ashes in a white coffin. But little or none of this was reported in the news.

Edwin Chota had seen it coming: perhaps someone would have to die before people listened. However, those closest to him say this wasn't what worried him the most. 'He said he'd already accepted it, that he might die at any moment,' says Margoth Quispe, a lawyer for the community. What worried Chota, the only leader who could read and write, was that no other Asháninka had enough education to take on the illegal loggers. 'That's why he was teaching the other leaders,' says Quispe. 'But now they're dead as well.'

Ergilia Rengifo, Chota's neighbour, who was widowed and became the new leader of Saweto, says she isn't afraid. She will go on defending the forest and reporting the illegal loggers, even if it means risking her life. There's just one thing that concerns her.

'The problem,' she told me, 'is that I can't read.'

GOLD

'Man's folly hath enhanced the value of gold and silver because of their scarcity; whereas nature, like a kind parent, hath freely given us the best things, such as air, earth, and water, but hath hidden from us those which are vain and useless.'

Thomas More
Utopia

'It has been said that Peru is a beggar sitting on a golden bench. If this phrase was intended to suggest voluntary poverty, and immense wealth within arm's reach, it was much mistaken.'

Jorge Basadre
Meditaciones sobre el destino histórico del Perú
('Meditations on the Historical Destiny of Peru')

Aside from stainless-steel pans and a platinum tooth, Máxima Acuña Atalaya doesn't own any valuable metal objects. No rings or bracelets or necklaces. No costume jewellery or precious stones. She struggles to understand the fascination people feel for gold.

One icy morning in 2015, Máxima Acuña is breaking rocks on a hillside with sharp, well-aimed blows, preparing to lay the foundation for a house. Despite being less than five feet tall, she can carry stones almost twice her own weight on her back and butcher a hundred-kilo ram in minutes. When she visits the capital of Cajamarca, the region in Peru's northern mountains where she's from, she feels scared the cars will run her over, and yet she's prepared to confront a moving backhoe loader to defend the land where she lives, and where there's plenty of water for her crops. She can't read or write, but she has stopped a mining company from throwing her out of her house. For peasants, human rights activists and environmentalists, Máxima is a symbol of courage and resistance. For those who think a country's progress depends on exploiting its natural resources, she's a stubborn and selfish peasant. Or worse: an ambitious woman trying to fill her pockets from a multimillion-dollar corporation.

'People say there's lots of gold under my land and the lake,' she says in her high voice, her jet-black hair pulled back in a plait and the pick in her calloused hands. 'That's why they want me out.'

This is Laguna Azul – the blue lake – but it looks grey. Here in the Cajamarca mountains, more than 4,000 metres above sea level, on the roof of the world, a thick fog hangs over everything, dissolving all the outlines. There's no bird-song to be heard, or tall trees or blue sky or flowers anywhere around, because they all die so quickly, frozen by the wind. There are no blossoms except the roses and dahlias Máxima Acuña has embroidered around the fuchsia neckline of her blouse. It's January. Her mud-and-stone hut with a tin roof is about to collapse from the rains. The cold gnaws at her flesh and bones in the night. She needs to build a new house, she says, but who knows if she'll manage.

A few metres away, beyond the cloud that envelops us, opposite her plot of land called Tragadero Grande, is the Laguna Azul, where a few years ago Máxima would fish for trout with her husband and four children. The Yanacocha mining company plans to drain that lake and deposit some 480 million tonnes of rock, mud and toxic waste in its place, 480 million tonnes of waste rock taken from a giant hole made by machines and dynamite.

Yanacocha, in Quechua, means 'black lake'. It was also the name of a lake that disappeared in the early 1990s to make way for a surface gold mine, considered in its heyday to be the biggest and most profitable in the world. Under the lakes of Celendín, the province in Cajamarca where Máxima and her family live, there is more gold. To extract it, the Yanacocha mining company drew up a project called Conga, which economists and politicians said would carry Peru into the First World: it would attract more investment, and therefore more jobs and modern schools and better hospitals and high-end restaurants and new hotel chains and, as President Humala announced in 2012, even a metro line in the capital. Although, to achieve all this, some sacrifices would have to be made. The Conga project would turn a lake a kilometre from Máxima's house into a surface mine. It would then deposit the mining waste in another two lakes nearby. One of those is the Laguna Azul.

If that happens, the peasant woman says, she could lose everything she owns: the almost twenty-five hectares of land full of ichu and other grasses fed by water from the springs; the pines and dwarf queñual trees that provide firewood; the potatoes, ollucos (a kind of root vegetable) and beans from her smallholding; and the water drunk by her family, her five sheep and four cows. Their former neighbours have sold their land to the company, and the Chaupe-Acuñas are the only family still living next to the mining project's future extraction zone: in the very heart of Conga. They swear they'll never leave.

'Some people in the community are angry with me, they say it's my fault they don't have work, that the mine's not up and running because I'm here. What am I supposed to do? Let them take my land and water away?'

Máxima stops splitting rocks and wipes her sweaty hands on her black woollen skirt.

Her fight with Yanacocha, she says, began with the building of a road.

Máxima woke up one morning burning with fever, and with stabbing pains in her stomach. She had an acute infection in her ovaries, and could barely get up from her mattress and walk. Her children hired a horse to take her down the hill to the hut they inherited from their grandmother in Amarcucho, a hamlet eight hours away, where she could recover. An uncle would stay and tend the smallholding. Three months later, in December 2010, when she felt better, Máxima and her family returned home, but they noticed something different about the landscape: the old dirt path that crossed part of their land had been turned into a wide, flat road. Their uncle told them some Yanacocha workers had come with bulldozers.

Máxima went to complain at the company offices, on the outskirts of Cajamarca. She persevered day after day until an engineer agreed to see her. From her woven bag, she produced a tattered piece of yellowing paper and showed it to him. It was her certificate of ownership.

'That land belongs to the mine,' she remembers him saying, as he eyed the document suspiciously. 'The Sorochuco community sold it fifteen years ago. Are you telling me you didn't know?'

Surprised and annoyed, the peasant woman had nothing but questions. How was that possible, if she'd bought the parcel of land from her husband's uncle in 1994? How was it possible, if she'd spent years looking after other people's cattle and milking cows to save up the money? She had paid two bulls for that land, worth almost $100 apiece. How could Yanacocha be the owner of Tragadero Grande if she had a piece of paper saying otherwise?

That afternoon, the company engineer sent her away from his office with no answers.

Half a year later, in May 2011, days before her forty-first birthday, Máxima Acuña set off at dawn to a friend's house to weave her a sheep's-wool shawl. On her return, she found her guinea-pig pens overturned. The potato and olluco plot destroyed. The stones her husband Jaime

Chaupe was collecting to build the new house scattered. Her hut reduced to a pile of ashes. The next day, Máxima and Jaime walked for hours down the hill to the Sorochuco police station to report Yanacocha.

'I've just spoken to the engineers and they say that land's been sold,' the police chief told them, after making them wait outside his office for five hours in the blazing sunshine.

'Maybe other people sold what's theirs, but not my land,' Máxima insisted, certificate in hand.

'Well, let's hope you didn't sell it, because if you did, you really are screwed.'

Máxima and Jaime refused to leave the police station until an officer wrote up their complaint. They were supposed to take that piece of paper to the Celendín public prosecutor's office, which they did, but it made no difference. A prosecutor from the province closed the complaint days later: there wasn't enough evidence to prove the mining company had attacked them.

Back in Tragadero Grande, the Chaupe-Acuñas had no choice but to build a temporary hut out of ichu grass and try to get on with their lives. Then August came. Máxima and her family recount what happened to them at the beginning of that month as a series of violations which they're afraid will be repeated.

It happened over five days.

On 8 August, a policeman showed up at the hut and kicked over the pans where they were stewing potatoes and boiling milk for breakfast. He told them they had to leave the land. They stayed put.

On 9 August, some police officers and Yanacocha security guards seized their possessions, pulled down the hut and set fire to it.

On 10 August, the family slept out in the open. They covered themselves with piles of ichu grass as protection against the cold.

On 11 August, a troop of police officers with helmets, riot shields, clubs and rifles came to throw them out. They brought a backhoe loader with them. Jhilda, Máxima's youngest daughter, fifteen years old, knelt in front of the vehicle to stop it entering the land. While some police officers beat her mother and siblings with clubs to get them out of the road, a sub-officer smacked Jhilda in the back of the neck with the butt of his gun, knocking her out. Ysidora, the older daughter, filmed the rest of the scene on her phone. The video lasts a couple of minutes and you can see it on YouTube: her mother is screaming; her sister is unconscious on the ground. The Yanacocha engineers watch from a distance, next to their white trucks. The troop of police officers, lined up in rows, is about to leave.

August the 12th was the coldest day of that year in

Cajamarca. The Chaupe-Acuñas spent the night in the pampas, in minus seven degrees.

The mining company has denied these accusations time and again, to judges and journalists. They demand proof. Máxima Acuña has medical certificates and photos that show the bruises they left on her arms and knees. That day the police wrote a report which accused the family of attacking eight sub-officers with sticks, stones and machetes, though it also recognises that these officers had no power to remove them without authorisation from a public prosecutor.

'Have you heard that the lakes are for sale?' asks Máxima, before hoisting a heavy rock onto her back. 'Or that the rivers are for sale and we're not allowed to use the spring?'

Since the press coverage, Máxima Acuña's struggle has won her supporters in Peru and abroad, but also sceptics and enemies. To Yanacocha, she is a usurper of land. To activists and thousands of peasants in Cajamarca she is the Lady of the Blue Lake, as they began to call her when word about her resistance spread. The old metaphor of David and Goliath was inevitable: it was the word of an Andean campesina against the most powerful gold-mining corporation in Latin America. Although what was at stake, really, affected everyone: the case of Máxima Acuña is the story of clashing visions of what we call progress.

Astrophysicists say that all the gold in the bowels of the earth, which we now feverishly exploit, came here from space 3.9 billion years ago – when the planet was a giant ball of magma – after a meteorite shower. Gold, the theory goes, would have fallen from the sky. And there's one thing we know for sure: no other mineral has seduced and disturbed people's imagination like that glinting metal whose chemical symbol is Au – from the Latin 'aurum', aurora, radiant dawn.

Any book of world history will show us that the hunger to possess it has led to invasions and wars, strengthened empires and religions, laid waste to mountains and forests, shaped the destinies of kings and emperors, inspired beautiful works of art and provoked horrific crimes. The God of Israel punished the Hebrews for worshipping a golden calf, and then ordered that the tabernacle where they worshipped him be made of the same material. The pharaohs believed that gold ensured their magnificence in the afterlife and demanded to be buried wrapped in the 'flesh of the gods'. Crassus thought he could buy Rome's military glory and died when he was forced to swallow molten gold. Christopher Columbus thought the gold from the Indies could finance a crusade to liberate Jerusalem from the infidels and thus earn him a place in Paradise. Once a year, the Inca ruler Pachacuti covered his body in gold dust, the 'sweat of the sun', and then bathed in Lake Titicaca to purify himself. The Spanish conquistador Francisco Pizarro died while dining in his Lima palace, run through by enemy swords, surrounded by the golden treasures he'd stolen. Newton devoted years to alchemy and studied how to turn ordinary metals into gold. The Genoese and Florentines made it into coins to express their economic power. Arab chiefs used gold to humiliate their rivals, coupling commercial acumen with military prowess. People from Britain and the United States built complex gold-based financial systems to shield themselves from devaluation and the protests of the poor. Bounty hunters threw John Sutter off his farm when his watermill sparked the California gold rush. Many an explorer perished in the Amazon rainforest hunting for a golden city called El Dorado. From King Midas, cursed by his greed, to Aga Khan III, who every year donated his weight in gold to his people; from the insalubrious mines of South Africa to the sterilised vaults of Fort Knox; from the street markets of Bengal to the financial markets of the City of London; from the exquisite goldwork of the Chimú people to the treasures of long-forgotten galleons in ocean trenches – that golden metal brought here by galactic rocks millennia ago has always reflected 'the universal quest for eternal life – the ultimate certainty and escape from risk', according to Peter L. Bernstein, a financial historian.

Gold is not vital to any living thing. It serves primarily to feed our vanity and illusions of security: more than fifty per cent of the gold extracted in the world ends up as jewellery that adorns millions of necks, ears, hands and teeth. Forty per cent is used as financial backup, in the form of bars and coins held in central banks. Nine per cent is used in the telecommunications industry (inside mobile phones, computers, televisions, GPS devices) and health sciences (the tests to diagnose malaria and HIV, as well as treatments for arteriosclerosis and cancer, use nanoparticles of gold). Beyond that, gold has fewer practical uses than other metals and alloys. With steel we can construct buildings, ships, cars, all kinds of machines. With gold, a soft mineral, it's not possible to forge tools or resistant weapons. Yet it's gold that we call a precious metal. Its main qualities – it never rusts, it never loses its shine – make it one of the most coveted metals of all. Long after steel has corroded and rusted, gold – being chemically inert – will remain unchanged. Gold survives the passage of time, the ravages of nature, human machinations. The problem is that there's less and less gold left to exploit.

Some people imagine that gold is extracted by the tonne and transported in hundreds of lorries in the form of ingots to high-security vaults, when in fact it's a rare metal. If we collected all the gold obtained throughout history – 187,000 tonnes, the World Gold Council estimates – and melted it down, it would barely fill four Olympic swimming pools. The richest reserves on the planet are running out and it's increasingly difficult to find new supplies. More than half of the gold that exists above ground has been mined in the past five decades. And the ore that has yet to be extracted is usually buried in tiny quantities beneath inhospitable mountains and lakes.

To end up with an ounce of gold – enough to make a wedding ring – you need to extract fifty tonnes of earth, or the contents of forty removal lorries. The landscape afterwards reveals a stark contrast: while the mining companies leave scars in the earth so vast they can be seen from space, the particles extracted are so minuscule that as many as 200 could fit on the head of a pin.

One of the last remaining gold reserves happens to lie under the hills and lakes of Cajamarca, where the Yanacocha mining company has been operating since the end of the twentieth century. The same Andean region where hundreds of peasants have lived for generations. Máxima Acuña is one of them. A woman who lives on top of a goldmine, but has never seen or touched a single nugget of that yellow metal which is of no use to her.

If anyone tried to visit Máxima Acuña, they might find their way blocked by an iron barrier. To reach her house, you have to take a minibus from Cajamarca and travel for four hours through valleys, hills and narrow chasms like ravines until you reach the area around Laguna Azul. This wouldn't be difficult, were it not for the checkpoint of the Conga mining project – which takes its name from the Quechua 'kunka', 'neck'. If you're from Lima or from outside Peru, they won't let you past. If you say you're going to see Máxima Acuña, they won't let you past, unless you take out a television camera. That lady's got problems with the mine, the guard in the orange jacket will say, walkie-talkie in hand. Then he'll make you get out of the vehicle and write your name down in a notebook, and you'll tell him this is a public road and he'll say again that no, sir, it's not possible, this route is only for members of the community. If you keep trying, he'll call the police who patrol the area in a white truck from the mining company. It's private property, they'll say. Then perhaps you'll pay the driver who brought you this far a little extra to take a detour and drive another two hours to Santa Rosa, the closest community to the Chaupe-Acuñas's house. It will be night by the time you arrive. In exchange for more money, a peasant will perhaps agree to give you a ride on his motorbike down a track full of puddles, until you're nearly at another checkpoint. Then you'll have to get off the motorbike and walk over a hill, in the dark, crouching down, so the Yanacocha guards don't see you. The motorbike is waiting on the other side. You carry on. Ten minutes later you reach Tragadero Grande. All around you is mud and grass and fog. Some dogs are barking. The darkness is so thick it seems to swallow the torchlight.

'We live like hostages here,' Máxima said the night I met her, stoking the fire to heat up a pan of potato soup. 'We can't go far, we can't have visitors, we can't walk where we want. It's very sad to live the way I do.'

Three decades before becoming the Lady of the Blue Lake, when she was still a girl, Máxima Acuña was terrified of the police. Every time she saw an officer on the streets of her town, she cried and clung to her mother's skirt. She was scared of those men in their oil-green uniforms and dust-covered boots. Máxima, the second-youngest of four siblings, was painfully shy. When visitors came to her home in Amarucucho – from the Quechua 'amarukuchu', 'corner of snakes' – she used to hide. She didn't have any friends. She didn't play with dolls, but she liked making clothes for the newborn babies in the neighbourhood.

Back then, in the early 1970s, Peru was governed by the military. For centuries the landowners had been masters of all that fell within their domain: mountains, lakes and rivers, as well as the indigenous peasants who worked there. Indigenous people essentially had no rights. They spent their lives working on their masters' farms, almost like slaves. A country like that is a ticking time bomb. One spring day in 1968, two years before Máxima Acuña was born, General Juan Velasco Alvarado led a coup. He punished the landowners, taking away their estates and handing them to the peasants. For the first time in centuries, they could own land themselves. According to the anthropologist Enrique Mayer, a professor at Yale University, this signified 'a momentous shift in the history of the Andes, akin to the abolition of slavery in the Americas'. The regime promised a nationalist revolution, and proclaimed: 'Land for those who work it.' That was the plan, the utopia.

In the mountains of Cajamarca, the young Máxima grew up under that new regime in which peasants, people like her, had come closer to being citizens. The reforms allowed her parents to acquire a small parcel of land in Amarcucho. Máxima spent her days weaving white straw hats, cleaning out the guinea-pig pens or collecting firewood and helping her mother on the smallholding. Her mother taught her to weave ponchos, shawls and skirts, which, as the years went by, she would sell in the markets. Her father died when she was eight and she was never sent to school. She was keen to grow up so that she could work, have her own smallholding and buy herself a pair of shoes. If she ever had children, she didn't want them to go around barefoot like her.

The years passed. Máxima's body changed, but not her personality. She didn't go to parties. She didn't talk to boys. 'The girl didn't talk to anyone, in fact,' recalls Jaime Chaupe, her husband, a sturdy, quiet man in his fifties with a wide nose. 'She was really stubborn and strong like a man.'

Jaime and Máxima got married when he was eighteen and she was sixteen. For the first years of their marriage, Máxima lived with her in-laws. Jaime's family – who were from the same hamlet, and owned some small parcels of land – made her get up at dawn to gather firewood, peel wheat and corn for the labourers and wash all the family's clothes. They insulted her, they beat her, they were ashamed that she couldn't read or write. That's why she was always very strict with her own children, to the point of keeping them shut up at home, banning them from having girlfriends or boyfriends and hitting them hard with a belt if they didn't do their homework.

'If you can't read, who's going to give you work in the city?' says Máxima, who used what she made from weaving and looking after cattle to send her children to study at the university in the city of Cajamarca. 'People with a profession are safe there. Not people like me.'

Máxima wanted to escape the unfair treatment she suffered from Jaime's family. And so, during the years she lived with them, while Jaime was away for weeks on end working on other smallholdings, she tended people's sheep and sold alforja bags and shawls she had woven, in order to save up enough money to buy her own land and live there with her children. And that's what she managed to do, but then the dispute with Yanacocha began.

Over the six years of court cases, appeals and hearings she went through after the company tried to evict her from Tragadero Grande, she learnt which other things she didn't want for herself. She decided, for example, that she would never live in a city. The first time she went to Cajamarca to report the destruction of her hut, she almost got run over twice because she didn't know what the red traffic lights meant. She learnt that the black smoke from the cars gives her a rash, that she finds the spaghetti in the restaurants disgusting, that she hates the taste of olives and can't go out alone because she always gets lost.

'Besides, everything's money there. Here, if I want food, I take my animals, I rent my animals out, or I go to the potato minga for two, three days, and they give me sacks of potatoes.[1] If I want meat, I kill a chicken, a guinea pig. Here I plant, I tend, I sew. In the city I feel horrible.'

During those years, she also realised she could express what she was feeling through songs. Máxima can sing. On the marches with other peasants and activists, there's always someone who encourages her to stand up before the crowd and improvise a yaraví – a sweet, melancholic Andean song – that tells the story of their struggle. When

1 The *minga* or *minka* – from the Quechua 'minccacuni', 'to ask for help promising something in return' – is a pre-Hispanic tradition of community work or voluntary collective action with a social purpose, or for mutual aid. They still occur today in various Latin American countries.

she began her fight with Yanacocha, she also learnt her own name. She'd always thought she was Maximina, as her mother used to call her. But when her lawyer read her ID, she told her that her real name was Máxima. Hers was a name without diminutives.

There's a popular saying that most Peruvians hear at some point, in the classroom or the street: 'Peru is a beggar sitting on a golden bench.' It's a metaphor – wrongly attributed to the Italian naturalist Antonio Raimondi – that speaks of the immense wealth of natural resources the country has at its fingertips, and from which, during the course of its history, whether from lack of vision or because of the corrupt political class, it has never been able to benefit. Or even worse: wealth that, for five centuries, *other people* have been exploiting right under its nose.

When, in 1532, Spanish boots landed for the first time on the Inca empire of Tahuantinsuyo, it was the largest empire on the planet: larger than the expanding Russia of Ivan the Great, larger than the powerful Great Zimbabwe on the West African plains, larger than the Ottoman Empire and the Aztec Empire, and far larger than any European state at the time.[2] Atahualpa, the last

2 In *1491: New Revelations of the Americas before Columbus* (2005), the writer and reporter Charles C. Mann notes that at one point Tahuantinsuyo stretched over thirty-two degrees of latitude, and

ruler of the Inca civilisation, was captured in Cajamarca by the Spanish conquistador Francisco Pizarro and his soldiers, just as he was ordering his half-brother's execution so that he could hold on to the throne. Atahualpa noticed that his captors had an irrational lust for gold. The Inca people didn't know about iron, glass or gunpowder. Nor did they use wheels. But they knew all about that yellow mineral: it was beautiful, easy to work, perfect for making jewellery and statues to honour their gods. But the invaders' obsession with gold – which couldn't be eaten, drunk or woven, and was too soft to make weapons or tools – was inexplicable to them. So Atahualpa reached up his arm as high as he could and drew a red line along his cell wall: in exchange for his freedom, he said, he would fill his cell to that line with gold and silver pieces: a treasure valued today at $1.5bn, the highest ransom ever paid in human history. Pizarro and his partners, however, shared out the booty and then strangled the Inca in front of his subjects.

From then on, while the Spanish soldiers were pillaging the gold from the New World so their aristocracy could squander it on silk, porcelain and spices from Asia,

included territory from modern-day Colombia, Ecuador, Peru, Bolivia, Chile and Argentina: as if a single power controlled all the land between St Petersburg and Cairo. In spite of its power, it was the shortest-lived empire: it lasted just a hundred years before being crushed by Spain.

Cajamarca became another region where wars, epidemics, slave labour in the mines and mestizaje (racial and cultural intermixing of Spanish and indigenous people) left a deep scar in the emotional memory of the native population. The metaphor of the beggar sitting on a golden bench became, for generations of Peruvians, an allegory of this plundering, which many would say has a contemporary equivalent: unhappy people watching very happy corporations blow up the land to extract gold.

Peru is the number one exporter of gold in Latin America and number six in the world, after China, Australia, Russia, the United States and Canada. This is due, in part, to the gold deposits it has and to investment from transnational companies like Newmont, which, as of June 2018, was the owner of fifty-one per cent of Yanacocha shares (the Peruvian company Minas Buenaventura and the Japanese Sumitomo Corporation own the rest).[3] Few multinationals have seen more aggressive

3 In October 2005, after a six-month investigation, the *New York Times* published an article headed 'Tangled Strands in Fight Over Peru Gold Mine'. In it, Jane Perlez and Lowell Bergman, Pulitzer winners, describe how the company Newmont gained control of the Yanacocha mine, following accusations of corruption and bribes. In 1994, during the Fujimori dictatorship, the original owners of Yanacocha were Newmont, the Peruvian company Buenaventura and the French company BRGM. The partnership ended when the French company tried to sell some of its shares to a competitor of Newmont's. Billions of dollars were at stake. The Denver giant turned to the Peruvian courts to stop them and, with the intervention

growth than the so-called Denver giant, which operates open-cast mines on five continents, from the plateaus of Ghana to the peaks of Peru. It creates jobs and brings basic services to remote corners of the globe, but it also boasts the dubious distinction of producing the most waste per ounce of the whole mining industry, coal mining included.

In one day, Yanacocha digs up around 200,000 tonnes of earth and rock, with which you could build three Cheops pyramids. Whole mountains disappear in weeks. An ounce of gold – enough for a pair of earrings – is worth around $1,300. Extracting that amount produces some twenty tonnes of waste, which includes chemicals and poisonous metals.

This waste is toxic because gold-mining companies, in a process called leaching, pile up the rock with the metal inside it and tip a solution of cyanide and water over the top, which then slowly trickles down, dissolving the rock around the gold as it goes. Cyanide is a deadly poison. An amount the size of a grain of rice is enough to kill a human being, and a millionth of a gram dissolved in a litre of water can kill dozens of fish in a river. Yanacocha, the owner of the biggest cyanide leaching mine in the country, insists that the cyanide remains inside the mine pit and is treated

of Fujimori's adviser, Vladimiro Montesinos, won the case in the Supreme Court of Justice.

according to very high safety standards. But many people in Cajamarca doubt the chemical processes are as clean as all that.

To prove their fears aren't unfounded or merely caused by anti-mining sentiment, they tell the story of Hualgayoc, a mining province over a hundred kilometres from Máxima Acuña's house, where the water in two of its rivers runs red and nobody swims any more. Or the story of San Antonio de Pachachaca, where a lake that supplied the community was contaminated by burnt oil leaking from the mine. Or of the town of Choropampa, where a lorry hired by Yanacocha accidentally spilt liquid mercury onto the highway and poisoned hundreds of families. In Choropampa, the mining company paid people to clean up the poisonous metal with no protective clothing. Women and children collected the mercury in little bottles and hid it in their homes, believing that the silvery liquid contained gold. Days later they suffered the consequences: dizziness, fever, vomiting. Peasants with spots on their skin, haemorrhaging, lying in hospital beds. Peasants who, seventeen years later, are still waiting for compensation.[4]

4 After the mercury spill in Choropampa in 2001, Newmont sent Lawrence Kurlander, the company's number-three executive at the time, to Peru, to carry out an environmental audit. Kurlander reported twenty serious high-priority problems in the Yanacocha mine, confirming the peasants' complaints: the water was polluted and the fish were disappearing. The findings were so serious –

Some kind of mining is necessary and unavoidable if we're to go on leading the comfortable lives we are used to. Our houses are made of cement, iron, sand and stone, and roofed with aluminium structures and sheets of zinc: all materials that come from open-pit mines. Our tiles, ceramic or marble, and our walls and windows with aluminium frames and glass, are also produced using mined substances. Not to mention all the electric wiring made of copper, the steel in cars, the spoon we bring to our mouth, and even the surgeon's scalpel as they operate on a damaged heart. However, mining, even at its most technologically advanced and least environmentally harmful, is considered a dirty industry all over the world. For Yanacocha, which has gained a bad reputation in Peru, cleaning up its image of environmental mishaps could prove as difficult as bringing the trout in a polluted lake back to life.

Community opposition worries mining investors, especially when it threatens a fall in profits. In 2015, Yanacocha estimated that there were only enough gold reserves in its other mines to last five more years. The Conga project – which would cover an area a quarter the size of Lima – would mean it could continue to operate, thanks to its more than six million ounces of gold reserves.

according to the October 2005 *New York Times* article – that Kurlander warned in a memo that the executive directors could be subject to 'criminal prosecution and imprisonment'.

In its environmental impact assessment, the mining company explains that it will drain four lakes, but also build four reservoirs. These reservoirs, it says, will collect more than enough rainwater to supply the 40,000 people who currently drink from the rivers that flow from those lakes. It will be extracting gold for nineteen years, but it will invest almost $5bn and employ some 10,000 people. Local and foreign executives will receive higher dividends. The state will collect more money in taxes to invest in roads, schools and other public works. People will have more and better jobs. That's their offer. The promise of prosperity for all.

Faced with that rosy picture, there is no shortage of politicians and economists ready to welcome the project with open arms, but there are also engineers and environmentalists who oppose it on public health grounds. Robert Moran, from the University of Texas, and Peter Koenig, a former World Bank economist, are water management experts. They have explained that the 20 lakes and 600 springs on the Conga site form an interconnected water system, a kind of circulatory apparatus created over millions of years. Damaging four lakes would affect the whole system forever.

Unlike elsewhere in the Andes, there are no glaciers in Peru's northern mountains to supply the people who live there with the water they need. In these mountains, the lakes form natural reservoirs. The black earth and the grasses serve as a huge sponge that absorbs rain and moisture from the mist. This then feeds the rivers and springs that irrigate the plains. In regions like Cajamarca – where forty per cent of the land could be allocated to mining – thousands of crop and cattle farmers like Máxima Acuña, increasingly well informed and well organised, fear that gold mining will pollute their only water sources.[5] They no longer trust the political leaders who promised to defend them.

One evening in early 2011, in the same region where Atahualpa was executed by his captors five centuries before, Ollanta Humala, then the left-wing presidential candidate in Peru, was wearing a traditional Cajamarca poncho and making a speech to a crowd in the Plaza de Armas.

5 In 2014, food safety experts from the University of Barcelona published the study 'Heavy metal and metalloids intake risk assessment in the diet of a rural population living near a gold mine in the Peruvian Andes (Cajamarca)'. This study found high levels of lead, cadmium and other heavy metals in the food and water of peasant communities near the Yanacocha mine. The largest amounts were found near the settlement of La Pajuela. These metals are linked to high rates of cancer, kidney failure and cardiovascular disease. 'It's reasonable to advise the inhabitants of La Pajuela not to drink from the water sources,' the report concluded. That same year, a report from the Ministry of the Environment warned that in the community of San José, near La Pajuela, contaminated water had leaked from the mine.

'I've seen a group of lakes and they say you want to sell them to the mining company. Do you want to sell your water?'

'Noooooooooo!'

'What's more important? Water or gold?'

'Waaateeerrr!'

'Because you can't drink gold, you can't eat gold. Our children drink water, our cattle drink water. And that's where we get milk, cheese, other riches. Water for the Peruvian people! And how are we going to defend it?'

The candidate Humala throws up his arms, grins, waves, is met with applause, shouts and more rapturous shouts.

One year after that speech, with the presidential sash across his chest, Humala confronted that same crowd in Lima. This time they were furious: he was supporting the Conga project. The new president declared a state of emergency in Cajamarca. People couldn't assemble freely. The police could enter houses without a legal permit. The repression of the protests ended with shots fired in Celendín that killed, among others, a boy of sixteen.

In Cajamarca and another two provinces affected by the Conga project, Humala's former supporters turned on him, calling him a traitor and a liar. The walls on some streets in Cajamarca city are painted with graffiti: 'Down with Conga', 'Water not gold'. In 2012, the tensest year of the anti-Yanacocha protests, the polling company Apoyo found that eight in ten people in Cajamarca were against the project. In Lima, where Peru's political decisions are made, the boom caused by international metal prices created the illusion that the country's pockets would go on filling with gold. But only if Conga went ahead. If not, some leading pundits warned, the consequences would be disastrous. 'If Conga doesn't go ahead, it will be like shooting ourselves in the foot,' wrote Pedro Pablo Kuczynski, who was running against Humala for the presidency at the time, in a column. For business executives, the Conga project would be a life raft in a crisis, a game-changing moment. For peasants like Máxima Acuña, it would mean making a few people rich at their expense. The peasants were still the beggars from that old metaphor.

Some say that Máxima Acuña's story is being used by anti-mining groups who don't want the country to develop. But local news has been tarnishing the optimism of those who want investment at all costs for a while now: in Peru, seven in ten social conflicts are caused by mining, according to the Peruvian human rights ombudsman. Official statistics show that Cajamarca is the region of the country which produces the most gold, but also the one with the most people living in poverty.

Máxima Acuña discovered she was brave when she saw police officers beating her children, in the first skirmish with Yanacocha. Before she became a symbol of social struggle, Máxima's hands would sweat and she'd feel nervous if she had to speak to an authority figure. After the attempts to evict her in 2011, she had to learn to defend herself before a judge.

That year, the mining company accused the Chaupe-Acuñas of the crime of 'aggravated usurpation'. According to the company's lawyers, the peasants attacked police officers and private security guards before invading the land. After that, the lawyer Mirtha Vásquez set about proving the innocence of Máxima and her family in the courts.

Vázquez is a petite woman from Cajamarca, forty years old, with pale skin, a small nose and straight hair the same dark shade as her eyes. As director of the NGO Grufides, she says, she has known many peasants mistreated by mining companies in Cajamarca, but she has never seen a woman who dared challenge the power of Yanacocha, especially not with the province's legal system against her.

'The public prosecutors in Celendín thought they were omnipotent,' recalls Mirtha, an environmental law specialist who tried to become a judge when she was younger, but was disillusioned to see so many corrupt judges and prosecutors in the courts. 'They mistreated Máxima and Jaime, they said they understood they'd committed crimes because they're uneducated people.'

The Chaupe-Acuña couple had to attend the hearings

– first in Celendín, the province where they live, and then in Cajamarca city – but they couldn't afford transport. So they woke up very early and walked for eight hours to the community of Sorochuco, where they caught a minibus that took them to the court. Usually, when they finally arrived, the judges would postpone the session because the Yanacocha representatives had said at the last minute that they couldn't make it.

In Cajamarca, Máxima's four children remained on the alert. When I met them in 2015, they were all living in a rented room with sky-blue walls, some thirty square metres in size, at the back of a dark, dusty carpentry workshop. That was where they ate, studied and slept, and they moved every now and then for safety. One night, two men in balaclavas threatened to kill Ysidora Chaupe as she was leaving the university where she studied accounting. Daniel Chaupe, her younger brother, who developed lung problems after the police officers hit him in the back with a club, was turned down for a job in a hardware shop. The owner said he'd never hire the son of an 'anti-miner'.

Meanwhile, in Tragadero Grande, Máxima and Jaime say they have faced harassment from the company. They say that Yanacocha's white trucks would park facing their land as often as six times a day; the security guards took photos, watched what the family were doing. One day a vehicle from the mine ran over two rams and its occupants stole two more. Another time they killed Mickey, the dog that protected the sheep from fox attacks and barked at anyone who approached their land. Some nights, the family say, they heard shots being fired. They all heard them. They wish they had a way of proving it.

The Chaupe-Acuñas lost two cases in the Celendín court. They were sentenced to almost three years in prison and instructed to pay nearly $2,000 to the mining company in compensation. They were told to leave the land they had 'invaded'. Vásquez, the lawyer, explains that the judges and public prosecutors didn't look at the proof the family presented, such as the certificate of ownership, the deed of sale and the statements from the relatives who sold them the land. Even the medical certificates detailing the blows they received during the first eviction were suspiciously mislaid in some provincial prosecutor's office. The family's lawyer appealed to the Superior Court of Cajamarca and a new trial began. During those months, with international help, Máxima Acuña and her eldest daughter travelled to Europe to tell their story and seek support.

Rocío Silva Santisteban, then executive secretary of the National Co-ordinator for Human Rights, recalls that the day before Máxima flew to Geneva to present her case to the United Nations, she spent the afternoon with Rocío in her Lima flat. When they went for a stroll along the Miraflores boardwalk, with its lush green parks, bridge and single lighthouse, Máxima took it all in with a mixture of curiosity and mistrust. She'd never seen people in such a hurry, or buildings so tall, and she'd never crossed such brightly lit avenues. She'd never seen the sea at night, and never from so close up. What intrigued her the most was how people in Lima managed to carry water up to the top floors of the buildings.

After her first international flight, Máxima landed in Switzerland – the country that buys the most gold from Peru – for a meeting with an official from the United Nations High Commission for Human Rights. In France she met with the metalworkers' union and a senator who went to visit her in Tragadero Grande a few months later. In Belgium, at a human rights forum, she heard about other women with similar stories to hers. Yolanda Oqueli, Guatemala: a mother of two, shot for leading peaceful protests against a mining project that would encroach on two communities. Carmen Benavides, Bolivia: threatened for opposing the industrial mining that pollutes the river where her ethnic group live. Francia Márquez, Colombia: persecuted by paramilitaries who wanted large-scale gold mining in her area. Francisca Chuchuca, Ecuador: denounced for opposing a gold-mining project that would contaminate two rivers that supply half a million peasants with water. In the narrative of modernisation, these women are the villains: each one of them has been accused of opposing progress.

Máxima Acuña says she's different to them in one respect: she's not interested in being an organiser or an activist, nor does she aspire to be a leader. 'I just want them to let me live on my land in peace, and not pollute my water,' she has said. But without intending to, the once timid woman who received the 2016 Goldman Prize (widely considered to be the environmental equivalent of the Nobel Prize) has become a source of inspiration for those who fight to stop the plundering of their land. 'She's one of the few people who haven't sold out to the mine,' says Milton Sánchez, secretary of the Inter-Institutional Platform of Celendín, who spent several nights in Tragadero Grande during the protests, along with hundreds of members of rondas (autonomous peasant patrols) and defenders of the lakes. Glevys Rondón, executive director of the Latin American Mining Monitoring Programme and Máxima Acuña's interpreter during her trip, says that unlike most defenders, who have a polished, articulate way of speaking, her Peruvian friend is very personal and intimate.

'In the world,' says Rondón, 'there are more people like Máxima.'

In 2003, a businessman reported the Argentinian José

Luis Godoy for allegedly usurping some land where he had lived for six decades, and which contained red granite quarries. In 2011, the police burned down the house of the Ecuadorian Alfredo Zambrano to dislodge him from the area of tropical rainforest where he lives and which the government expropriated to build a reservoir. In 2012, some hitmen blinded the son of the Venezuelan woman Carmen Fernández, after she fought to stop her ethnic group's land being handed over to coal-mining companies. In 2014, the Nicaraguan Fredy Orozco was accused of being a guerrilla when he wouldn't let the police remove him from his farmland in order to build an interoceanic canal. All of these people, like Máxima Acuña, have been accused of sacrificing their country's development for personal gain; of playing the victim in front of the cameras to take advantage of corporations; of being manipulated by NGOs that have their own agenda. Some people call them terrorists.

Máxima says she just wants to live the life she knows, the life that belongs to her: growing potatoes, milking cows, weaving woollen shawls, drinking the water from her springs and fishing for trout in the Laguna Azul without a guard telling her that 'this is private property'. She'd rather not have to fight. That's why, when she's asked to describe what the mining company has done to her, sometimes she refuses. She says that during the meetings in Europe she repeated her story ten times a day. It left her so fed up and depressed that when she got back to her hotel all she could do was sleep.

Her health collapsed when she returned from her trip. During those months, with the ongoing uncertainty over the court case, Máxima's head felt as heavy as a rock, her bones ached and she suffered from dizzy spells and fainting. Rocío Silva Santisteban, from the National Co-ordinator for Human Rights, took her to see a doctor. The diagnosis: severe stress aggravated by menopausal symptoms. She needed rest. They prescribed her sleeping pills, medication, hormones. She was given psychotherapy. She stopped doing interviews. While Máxima was building up her strength, ready for her third trial in Cajamarca, Yanacocha increased its legal team to six and hired Arsenio Oré Guardia, an eminent figure in Peruvian criminal law and an adviser to other mining companies like Barrick and Doe Run. Mirtha Vásquez admits to feeling intimidated at the prospect of litigating against Oré Guardia, the author of books she had studied obsessively at university. They had already lost two cases, and now they risked losing against one of the country's most distinguished lawyers. One morning in 2014, Vásquez gathered the Chaupe-Acuña family in her office. She wanted to be honest with them: the upcoming ruling, she said, was their last chance to win. If they lost, the family should consider moving elsewhere.

If they stayed, their lives would be in danger. Máxima told her she would stay there to die.

What goes through your head after a judge finds you innocent? When, at the end of 2014, the Superior Court of Cajamarca cleared her of the charge of illegally occupying Tragadero Grande, Máxima Acuña decided to get on with her life. She thought Yanacocha would finally leave her alone. She and her family chose a hill sheltered by a mountain 200 metres from her house to build a new home, because the one she had was about to collapse from the rains. Jaime and Máxima dug ditches, sipping fermented sugar-cane juice and chewing coca leaves to combat the exhaustion and cold. With the help of friends from their community, they collected stones for the bases and began building walls out of clay. But a few weeks after they laid the first stones, Yanacocha staff and security personnel entered the land with picks and spades to destroy the foundations. Máxima, Jaime, and two kids who were helping to build the walls at the time, tried to defend themselves with stones. The mining company's security drove them back with clubs. That afternoon, Yanacocha shared a video of what happened. They said that the land where the Chaupe-Acuñas were building wasn't part of the litigation, and that they had acted to defend their property. Máxima's lawyer disagreed with

Yanacocha, explaining that the court ruling applied to all the land in Tragadero Grande. She said the company had been trying to intimidate the Chaupe-Acuñas. The Cajamarca police – who had signed an agreement, still in force today, to provide security to the mine – didn't intervene. A squad of sub-officers stood on one side of the road, at the edge of the land, observing from a distance as Yanacocha used picks to destroy in minutes what the Chaupe-Acuñas had built.

At the Yanacocha mining company headquarters in Lima, there are offices called Perol, Chica, Mamacocha and Azul. They are named after lakes that could disappear as a result of the Conga project's gold extraction. The chemist Raúl Farfán is the company's director of external relations, and his office is next to those rooms. He's a young man with gelled hair and watchful eyes who receives me one morning in his apartment in Chacarilla, an elegant residential neighbourhood of the city. His job, among other things, involves ensuring good relations between the mining company and the communities. For the past twenty years, he has worked in corporate social responsibility for multinationals like Shell, Antamina and Xstrata, and he told me he understood why people were suspicious of Yanacocha – 'It's normal to side with the underdog in these cases' – but that not everything in the family's statements was true.

'We didn't destroy their house,' said Farfán, who had been in his post for ten months when I informed him of what happened in Tragadero Grande. 'We just removed the foundations of a new building so they don't go on invading our land.'

To better explain the reasons behind this decision, the chemist opened a map of the properties on his laptop. On it were marked two pieces of land bought by the Conga project from the Sorochuco community in 1996 and 1997. The Tragadero Grande area, which Máxima and her family claim is theirs, would have been included in those purchases. The Sorochuco management committee signed the sale documents. Samuel Chaupe, Máxima Acuña's father-in-law, signed as well, and guaranteed the transfer of the land. And in fact, said Farfán, there are satellite photos which prove that the Chaupe-Acuñas are lying when they say they have lived there since 1994. In the Google Earth images the executive showed me, there were no huts or smallholdings. According to the company, the family didn't 'invade' the land until 2011, when the Conga conflict began. Yanacocha says that the certificate of ownership 'the lady' showed is not a property title. Only the Sorochuco community, which did have titles, could sell the land. This is why the company reported the family and asked the police to remove them. This is its story.

'In building the new house, they were carrying out a

new invasion,' said Farfán. 'If you see a stranger building on your property, you have the right to remove the foundations within fifteen days. That's what the law says. We were defending our property.'

Days later, on an afternoon of torrential rain in Cajamarca, Miguel Ayala, who was president of the Sorochuco community when the first piece of land was sold to the Conga project, tells me that the company's version of events is distorted.

'The mining company says the family invaded, but how is that possible if twenty years ago I signed the certificate of ownership for their land and gave it to the Chaupes?'

Sitting in a corner of his grocery shop, Ayala explains that the Chaupe-Acuñas, like so many other peasant families, decided to move higher up the mountains, where Tragadero Grande is, to set up smallholdings and raise cattle. Back then, in the early 1990s, Peru was in the throes of a political and economic crisis. The war between the military and the Shining Path terrorists was strewing the country with the bodies of dead peasants. Banks and foreign companies were unwilling to invest. In Cajamarca, the plots of land in the lower areas yielded less and less as a result of the droughts, which grew ever more severe. Population growth meant less land was available for farming. Meanwhile, in the highest parts of the mountain range there were large, uninhabited areas of land, with access to water, and only foxes, pumas and chinchilla-like viscachas living there. What's more, Ayala says, they were worth almost nothing because, at the time, the mine didn't exist.

That was when Máxima and Jaime decided to go and live in Tragadero Grande, the parcel of land which at the time belonged to Jaime's uncle. Tragadero Grande was part of a much larger piece of land owned by the Sorochuco peasant community. The uncle sold them what he owned, and they signed a deed of sale. In January 1994, a year after Yanacocha produced its first gold bar, the community's management committee gave the Chaupe-Acuñas a certificate of ownership. After that, Ayala recalls, the couple would come down from their land to Sorochuco to barter: they'd bring sacks of potatoes and ollucos and exchange them for peas and corn, which other members of the community, like him, produced.

In the Andean world, there is a long tradition of land transfer under peasant norms. Alejandro Diez, an anthropologist who specialises in rural organisations, explained to me that, in Peruvian law, a peasant community is defined as an organisation of families who inhabit and control land, and who are linked by ancestral, social, economic and cultural ties. The members of the community have no individual property deeds: the land belongs to all of them. If you were born in the community, are the child of a community member or have been accepted as a member yourself, you're allocated a parcel and given a certificate of ownership. This is the equivalent, for them, of a property title. If you're the owner of the parcel and you want to leave, the land must be returned to the community. By now, however, it's become traditional to sell what you own to another peasant. In the Peruvian Andes, where there are more than 6,000 peasant communities, land is occupied and worked and inhabited this way. 'Modern Peru', however, is governed from the cities, and land is bought and sold independently of how it's used, worked and inhabited. Land is a possession, just another product. Law versus customs. Máxima Acuña and her family seem trapped in a crevasse between these two ways of seeing the world.

'It's a mess created by a precarious state,' Diez explained to me in his office in the Pontifical Catholic University of Peru. 'It remains to be seen who's legally in the right, the family or the company. I wouldn't be surprised if they both had rights.'

Yanacocha claims that its property titles – which on its maps include Tragadero Grande – are backed up by law, and it's true. But there are reports which claim that the land it currently owns, acquired in the early 1990s, belonged to communities and families who were pushed to sell under pressure of expropriation. Many peasants, impoverished and uneducated, say they weren't aware that the rocks under their fields contained immense wealth. Others say their neighbours fraudulently sold land which belonged to them.[6]

Miguel Ayala says he received an average of ten per cent of the real value of each hectare he sold. High up in Celendín, Máxima was the neighbour of her father-in-law, Samuel Chaupe, who did in fact sign the document that gave his land to the Conga project in a Sorochuco general assembly. Samuel sold his land off cheaply because he needed money for an operation on his youngest son. A heavy beam had smashed his head open while he was building a house.

'That's something real, something honest,' Ayala told me. 'Máxima and Jaime didn't sign the paper, so they didn't sell their land.'

The dispute between Máxima Acuña's family and the mining company was complicated not only by the legal loopholes, but also by numerical and geographical disagreements. In 2012, in the early days of the dispute between the Chaupe-Acuñas and Yanacocha, an expert from the Cajamarca regional government, the civil engineer

6 In their 2014 report *Large-Scale Mining: Do They Pay the Taxes They Should? The Yanacocha Case*, the journalists Raúl Wiener and Juan Torres show that, for a total of 20,609 hectares, Yanacocha paid $1,073m: just over $52 per hectare. The study estimates the economic damage to peasant families in Cajamarca at around $10m.

Carlos Cerdán, travelled to the contested land of Tragadero Grande.

Cerdán, a slight man in his forties with an angular nose and thick glasses, is a map specialist. He spent a morning marking out the exact area of the land using three GPS devices, the National Map and the boundaries set out in both parties' deeds of purchase. His study concluded that the parcel acquired by the Chaupe-Acuñas – almost twenty-five hectares – would not have been included in the land bought by Yanacocha. Or at any rate, Cerdán explained to me, that only a part of it would fall within the company's land, but not the whole parcel. This is because, although the limits are set out clearly in both sides' documents, there are problems with the calculations, and approximate measurements. It's all a jumble of figures and papers that don't reflect reality. No map is infallible.

'But we all make mistakes,' the engineer said. 'It could even be that I'm wrong.'

At no point in the trial was Cerdán's study considered. Lawyers for both sides have accepted that to resolve the dispute it will be necessary to go to a civil court, where each side will present evidence to show who the rightful owner is. However, Yanacocha says that even if this happens, it won't allow Máxima and her family to build a new house.

'We want to avoid land being invaded systematically,

another family coming along and wanting to invade,' says Raúl Farfán, the Yanacocha director. 'We don't want to set a dangerous precedent for the country.'

Modern politics, according to the French philosopher Paul Virilio, is about the administration of public fear. When people talk about the Conga project, some fear the land and water will be polluted. Others, that street unrest will break out and the investors will be scared away. The metaphors of progress – and its enemies – change depending on who uses them.

Weeks before I visited the chemist Farfán, Wilby Cáceres, the mining company's legal director, had been more emphatic about his concerns. According to him, the area where the Chaupe-Acuñas were trying to build another dwelling was inhabited by anti-mining leaders during the protests against the Conga project. 'We're worried the property will be occupied by them,' Cáceres told me over the phone. Although other Yanacocha executives wouldn't say as much into a Dictaphone, there's clearly another reason too: for as long as Máxima Acuña and her family are there, even if the company wins over local residents, the Conga project won't be able to go ahead.[7]

7 For the documentary *The Curse of Inca Gold* (2005), co-produced by PBS *Frontline* and the *New York Times*, Lowell Bergman interviewed Roque Benavides, then the executive president of Buenaventura and the owner of a forty-three per cent share in Yanacocha. When he asked about the social licence (permission from a community for a

At six in the morning in Tragadero Grande, a timid sun peeps out between the hills, gradually revealing what the dawn mist had kept hidden. A mud house. Some chickens wandering here and there. A wood stove where milk is boiling in a soot-blackened pan. A battery-powered radio resting on a rock. A radio station called Tigre, popular with Seventh-Day Adventists, plays huayno folk songs with violins and harps. A few metres away, the Lady of the Blue Lake, in her wide-brimmed straw hat, is watching her sheep on the pampas.

It's a month since I saw her breaking rocks and carrying them on her back on that hillside, and now the land we're walking on is covered in debris: mud, straw and wood, all damp from the rain. This is what's left over from the eviction; the remains of what would have been their new house. Next to them, a stone's throw away, the Yanacocha mining company has installed a long wire-mesh fence around a meadow of grazing alpacas. Inside the meadow is a guard post directly facing Máxima's house. One of the guards came over a few days ago to offer

company to exploit the resources in their area), Benavides, one of the most powerful executives in Peru, said: 'I hate the term "social licence". I do not understand what "social licence" means. We essentially apply social responsibility, caring for people. But a "social licence" – I expect a licence from the authorities, from the Minister of Mines. I expect a licence from the regional government. But I don't expect a licence from the whole community.'

her husband work. He told her Yanacocha didn't want to fight any more.

'Now they want peace, dialogue. As if I'm just some object they can do what they like with.' Máxima raises her voice, looking at the alpaca guard wrapped in his scarf. 'They say I've sold my land, I've run out of money. They say I'm shameless, wicked, a scrounger. That's how they've defamed me. They've beaten my children. Now they want to give us work. I'd rather be broke. My land makes me happy, and money doesn't.'

Around that time, various newspapers mentioned the existence of some property titles showing that the Chaupe-Acuña couple owned nine other pieces of land – almost eight hectares in total – in the hamlet of Amarcucho, one of the poorest in Cajamarca. These reports gave the impression that the family frequently turned up on empty pieces of land, occupied them and then appropriated them. In other words, they presented Máxima Acuña as a professional usurper. Ysidora Chaupe, Máxima's eldest daughter, recalls that after the news reports were published she received dozens of calls from people who supported her cause, including her own lawyer, who asked if she really did have more land, and why she hadn't mentioned it before.

'The other day an uncle phoned up and said: "Stop causing so much trouble, use your head and tell your parents to leave well alone",' Ysidora told me, while breastfeeding Máximo Salvador, her newborn son. 'They're saying my mum's a landowner, that she worked in a Chinese restaurant in Lima. But it doesn't matter if people don't believe us. We've got the papers. We declared it all in the trial.'

In Máxima Acuña's deeds of sale, that land appears as an inheritance from her parents and purchases from her siblings, for which she paid in rams or bulls. It's made up of scattered parcels, located on different hills. On some there's grass, on others there's firewood – or corn, or peas, which can only grow when it rains. It's estimated that a peasant family in the Peruvian mountains needs to own thirty-two hectares of land to produce the same as they could with one hectare of land on the coast, because of the challenges involved. Tragadero Grande, Máxima says, is the only place she owns where she can live, because it has plenty of grass, enough space to keep cattle and, most importantly, unlike the other pieces of land, water sources: there are springs all over it.

'The thing is, having some plots of land in Amarcucho doesn't make you rich,' laughed Miguel Ayala, Máxima's former neighbour, who has lived there for more than half a century. 'It's ridiculous.'

Nonetheless, some media outlets accused the lawyer Mirtha Vásquez and Grufides, the NGO she runs, of falsely portraying the Chaupe-Acuña family as victims. They say Vásquez is immoral and a liar. They have even, the lawyer tells me, broken into her house twice to smash all her things. She can't be sure who it was, but she has her suspicions, because they didn't take anything.

'They had to get back at us somehow,' says Vásquez, who is also a university professor and the mother of two children. 'Yanacocha won't forgive us for beating them in court. I'm just afraid for Máxima and her family. Sometimes I think this is costing us more than twenty-five hectares of land are worth.'

In the years that followed, Yanacocha accused the Chaupe-Acuña family of usurpation another ten or so times.[8] It has reported them for digging a potato plot, for planting pine trees on the boundaries, for herding sheep on another part of the land, and even for burning ichu grass to summon the rain, as is the custom among the peasants in the region. Now there's a metal fence on one side of her land which cuts them off from the road to Sorochuco, where they go to barter or buy food. Every so often a drone flies over the land. The community members and activists defending the Cajamarca lakes have arranged to go there

8 In May 2017, the Supreme Court of Justice, the highest court in Peru, ruled that Máxima Acuña and her family did not take violent possession of Tragadero Grande. The Yanacocha mining company respected the judgment, but said it would continue to claim ownership of the land in the civil courts.

and stand guard from time to time to protect the family. The regional governor of Cajamarca, Porfirio Medina, said in 2015 that if anything happens to the peasant woman 'the people will fight all the battles against the mining company's violations'. Máxima insists that even if the owner of Yanacocha himself came to apologise, it wouldn't make her forget everything she's been through.

'It's planted within me.'

Heavy rain suddenly begins to fall over Tragadero Grande. On Radio Tigre a woman sings about God's forgiveness, a balm for the soul. Máxima Acuña hangs the radio over her shoulder and quickens her pace in her rubber boots to get back to her hut. A skinny white dog bounds alongside her, barking non-stop.

'His name's Johnny,' the peasant tells me, with an ironic chuckle.

She chose it 'in honour' of the Yanacocha guard who burned down her first hut, whose name is Johnny as well.

On one of my last visits to Tragadero Grande, days before the foundations of Máxima's new house were destroyed, I saw the Yanacocha security trucks arrive and park outside the land. Around noon, some guards, accompanied by police officers with helmets, clubs and shields but no ID, entered the smallholding to take photos and videos of the walls of the house the couple were building.

Máxima and Jaime ran towards the hill from which the men were approaching. Máxima used her mobile to call a local radio station as she chased after the police, shouting: 'You're animals!' I ran over to them. I asked one of the police officers why they'd entered the land, who had given the order. I said I was a journalist. He didn't respond. I began taking photos, recording the scene on my phone. Then a burly, dark-skinned guy in a blue jacket, who seemed to be in charge of the Yanacocha guards, waved his arm, telling them to back off and return to the trucks parked by the roadside. I followed. I asked the man in the blue jacket to please tell me his name. But he just turned to look at me from a long way off and yelled:

'You shouldn't be here!'

That night, wrapped in blankets and sitting on a couple of mattresses, the peasant couple and I ate our dinner of noodle soup in silence. When we finished, Máxima collected the plastic plates, while Jaime chewed coca leaves and smoked one cigarette after another. From a hollow in the mud wall, a dying candle gave off a faint light.

'Something bad is going to happen, my coca's gone bitter,' murmured Jaime, a superstitious man. He spat something green onto the ground. 'I don't know . . . All this fighting and fighting. Sometimes I just want to get out of here.'

The rain beat down on the tin roof as if trying to break it.

'Don't be afraid,' said Máxima. 'Those policemen don't scare me.'

Then she lay down next to Jaime and blew out the candle with one breath.

OIL

'Oil expresses perfectly the eternal human dream of wealth achieved through lucky accident, through a kiss of fortune and not by sweat, anguish, hard work. In this sense oil is a fairy tale and, like every fairy tale, a bit of a lie.'

Ryszard Kapuściński
Shah of Shahs

'People pay a high price for the false painting of happiness.'

Elias Canetti
Aufzeichnungen 1973–1984
('Notes 1973–1984')

If God could grant Osman Cuñachí one wish, he would ask for a smartphone. Or a football. Or to swap his plastic flip-flops for some neon trainers. In fact, thinking about it, he'd ask for a brick-and-mortar house like the ones he saw once in Lima, more resistant to storms than the leaf-thatched wooden huts of which there are so many in Nazareth. Which is why Osman, an Awajún boy, eleven years old, thin as a wire, in a faded Spiderman T-shirt, plans to move to the capital to study architecture, and have a wife and just one child, because he knows that raising three or four or five, as is common in his village, means a life of hunger and poverty. That's what he was told by his dad, a retired teacher who feeds five mouths with his monthly pension of 400 soles (about $130) – not even half the minimum wage. His father would prefer Osman to be a chemical engineer and learn all about oil, so that he can do better in life than he himself has. Because ever

115

since a huge broken pipe spilt around 500,000 litres of that fuel here, in this patch of humid, mountainous forest in Amazonas, the second-poorest region of the country, some adults have been saying that one month spent cleaning oil from the river pays seven times what you could earn farming the land. Although they worry that they may have been poisoned.

It's a rainy afternoon in June 2016, six months after he waded into a river full of oil, and Osman Cuñachí, a member of the largest indigenous nation in Peru's northern rainforest, is frowning and feeling weird as he looks at a huge poster of his face outside the communal house. This is where the Awajún people usually discuss important village business: selecting a leader, building a road, punishing a thief. The poster is advertising a health campaign, run by the National Co-ordinator for Human Rights and other NGOs, to test twenty-five boys and girls said to have fallen ill after collecting oil in exchange for money. The Osman in the picture is just under five feet tall, with black smears covering his face, arms and feet, and wearing a red T-shirt with the word 'Peru' emblazoned across it in white letters. He's smiling and holding a dirty bucket.

'You look gross,' jokes his friend, a spiky-haired boy in a Barcelona shirt, with a football under his arm. Osman hides his face in his hands.

The photo he finds so embarrassing, and which will be

the focus of outraged discussion in the country and the international press, was taken on a neighbour's phone the day Nazareth went from being Bagua province's largest community – with its 4,000 inhabitants, brown river and millions of towering trees – to being the centre of 'the worst ecological disaster of the past decade'.

The afternoon he got covered in oil, Osman Cuñachí was practising free kicks with his friend when two engineers from Petroperú, the country's most profitable state enterprise, pulled into Nazareth in a white 4x4 truck. Since early that morning, corrosive fumes had been rising from the banks of the Chiriaco river and filtering into the wooden huts like an invisible cloud of petroleum. An eleven-centimetre crack in a corroded stretch of the North Peruvian Pipeline – a steel snake that transports oil from the rainforest to the coast, over a distance of more than 800 kilometres – had spilt enough oil into a nearby stream to fill almost half an Olympic swimming pool. Locals hired by Petroperú built a makeshift barrier from logs and tarpaulins that contained the crude for a few days, but no one had reckoned on a violent storm in the early hours making it overflow and ooze downstream like black phlegm, swallowing all the insects, tree roots, canoes, and plantain, cacao and peanut plantations in its path. The animals fled as it advanced. Mothers wept next to their ruined smallholdings. Dead fish floated on the dark water.

Fourteen oil spills contaminated the Peruvian rainforest in 2016, caused by that metal boa constrictor with a tendency to shed its own blood. Nazareth was the first link in a chain of catastrophes.

In his sixth-grade science textbook, Osman Cuñachí had read that oil is a prehistoric substance, made from the same material as dinosaur fossils. And in an episode of *Tom and Jerry* he'd seen it come gushing up from the bowels of the earth, an unstoppable black torrent that made whichever lucky person found it jump for joy. But he only learnt that oil was worth money on the afternoon of the spill, when the Petroperú engineers showed up in their 4x4 and announced to the families that they'd pay anyone who helped collect the fuel from the river.

While farming plantains could make someone around 20 soles ($6) a day, collecting oil in a bucket could earn them 150 soles: twice the salary of a doctor in the Amazonas region. In an area where seven in ten people are poor, where there's no drinking water or toilets, where the women suffer from anaemia caused by chronic malnutrition, where a child under five is more likely to die of malaria than from being bitten by a snake, where cold winds and unexpected droughts make it difficult to find fertile land to farm, the payment from Petroperú was more than an Awajún could imagine earning in a week.

The engineers didn't say it would be dangerous. They

didn't give out protective clothing or explain who should and shouldn't do it. That afternoon, whole families went to the river to collect as much oil as they could.

When Osman Cuñachí and his three siblings reached the polluted river, they saw children, pregnant women, grandmothers and young men wading in the water or sitting in canoes, scooping oil into buckets and plastic bottles. The same river where they usually bathed and built mud castles on the banks, where they'd learnt to swim and catch boquichicos and catfish, now gave off a metallic odour that made them feel sick. Their throats tickled. Their eyes streamed. Roycer, Osman's four-year-old brother, was the first to quit. Then seven-year-old Omar, and Naith, his fourteen-year-old sister. Immersed in the black waters, Osman decided to stay until he'd filled up his bucket, unaware that this flammable liquid sticking to his hands was what enabled entire cities to function.

We hardly give oil a second's thought, except for noting the acrid smell at petrol stations when we're filling the tank with diesel. But oil isn't something we can separate from ourselves, by standing away from the pump and holding our nose. Thanks to its power and the industries derived from it, for the past century it has underpinned our whole way of life. Heating our buildings and running our machines and vehicles – think of a television factory, or the plane we take to go on holiday – consumes eighty-four per cent of the oil extracted annually worldwide. The remaining sixteen per cent is transformed into the raw materials for manufacturing millions of things. Without this black gold – and the modern-day alchemy that takes place in oil refineries – it would be impossible to chew gum or drive a car, and there would be no such things as trainers, or toothpaste, or deodorant, or contact lenses, or tarmac roads, or tyres, or wheelie suitcases, or perfume, or lipstick, or sunglasses, or detergent, or mouthwash, or moisturiser, or false teeth, or sports shirts, or disposable razors, or nylon tights, or Teflon pans, or hair gel, or nail varnish, or sun cream, or umbrellas, or rubbish bags, or prosthetic heart valves, or aspirins, or cancer drugs, or crop fertilisers, or preservatives for food, or polystyrene cups, or lubricant for sex, or vitamin tablets, or fibre optics, or cement, or toothbrushes, or shampoo, or shower curtains, or hosepipes, or laptops, or photographic paper, or soap, or hair dye, or ballpoint pens, or the ink for printing books, or X-ray machines, or bottles of mineral water, or artificial flowers, or tablecloths, or carpets, or glue, or wigs, or matches, or fire extinguishers, or life jackets, or dynamite, or false eyelashes, or toilet seats, or music CDs, or headphones, or baths, or shirt buttons, or toilet paper, or condoms, or almost anything else made of plastic: from spaceship parts to Barbie dolls; from footballs to any of the almost three billion smartphones there are in the world, like the one that Osman Cuñachí, the Awajún boy, thought about buying with the money the Petroperú engineers promised in exchange for his bucket of oil.

It was dark by the time Osman and his siblings got back to their wooden house. Their mum gave them a telling-off as soon as she saw them, for going out without permission. Then they ran into the yard, where the clothes were hanging up and the chickens were clucking, and tried to get rid of the oil with soap and water, but they couldn't. They switched to washing-up liquid and it was no better. They scrubbed their faces, arms and legs with a scrubbing brush and laundry detergent. Nothing worked. Then a cousin, who'd been in the river as well, suggested they wash with motorcycle fuel. That night Osman couldn't sleep properly because his skin was itchy and burning from all the scrubbing. The next morning, the Petroperú engineers came back to Nazareth in their 4x4. The air still reeked of petrol. Some thirty Awajún residents were waiting by the roadside with their buckets full of oil. They had been offered 150 soles ($46) for each container. But in the end, despite people's complaints, the engineers only paid 20 soles ($6). Osman remembers that an engineer asked him how old he was, wrote his name down in a notebook and gave him 2 soles (about 60 cents), as pocket money for the bucket he'd collected: it was more water than oil, the engineer said. Osman, whose name means 'docile as a baby bird', didn't protest like the other children. When he got home, he gave one coin to his mum and with the other he went with his friends to buy a Pepsi and a bag of animal crackers.

And one day, just like that, you're a child who's become news. Everyone's interested in you, but almost no one knows anything about you. Newspapers, TV channels and NGO delegations travel for twenty-three hours from Lima by road, across the Andes, negotiating dizzying curves and warm valleys flanked by walls of vegetation, until they reach Nazareth, the indigenous community where you were born. They want to meet you. They look at you, and ask: Were you afraid? How did you wade into the river? Where are your oil-stained clothes? Can you show me? It's like they're competing to see who can recount the most horrible thing, knowing that the people most interested in these tragedies are those who have never experienced them, who live in plastic-addicted cities, relieved not to be you. The boy smeared with oil.

'My dad says people only come here when bad stuff happens,' says Osman Cuñachí, looking at his photo on the sign in his village. 'I want them to see me saving penalties, I don't want them to feel sorry for me.'

At six in the evening, the sky over Nazareth is a very dark purple. To say it's raining would be an understatement:

rain here means unstoppable torrents of water combined with blustering winds that make the roseapple trees shake. The tin roof of the communal house is leaking and the droplets form little puddles on the floor. There's no electric light because of a problem with the generator, and Dr Fernando Osores, a tall, thickset man in his forties, is straining to see in the gloom. He's taking blood and urine samples and cutting locks of hair from twenty-five Awajún boys and girls, aged between six and fifteen, who had collected oil from the river six months before.

While the parents sign permission forms, their children go, one by one, into a tent set up inside the house. The doctor from Lima takes the samples, which he will then send off to the laboratory of the Canadian Institut National de Santé Publique du Québec to be analysed. Under national health legislation, Peruvian state doctors were supposed to analyse the results the day after the spill. Six months have passed – and then a year will pass, and another – and nothing. 'They must be very busy,' Dr Osores says with a false smile. Suddenly a skinny boy comes racing out of the consulting room, terrified of the needles. His dad shouts something in Awajún and runs after him. The doctor, dripping with sweat, asks someone to hold his phone, with its torch on, so he can see what he's doing.

Osman Cuñachí isn't one of the children who have sat down to wait. When the rain subsides, he passes the time with his friends and his black dog Lucky on a patch of level ground outside, hunting scorpions and other insects, which he will then burn alive with a match. A few metres away, Jaime Cuñachí, Osman's father, aged sixty-six, spends the day sitting on a wooden stool, weaving a fishing net. A grey hat covers his bald head. His green shorts reveal a stump where his right leg used to be. It was amputated two years ago because of gangrene, which had been caused by his diabetes, a common disease among the Awajún, and difficult to treat because of poor diet and lack of medicine.

'I may be missing a leg but I've got a good memory,' chuckles Mr Cuñachí, a former chief of Nazareth, showing the few teeth he has left, as he swats mosquitoes away from his face with a rag.

He says the football pitch where his son now plays is a graveyard of old pipes and machinery, which were used in the late 1960s to build the North Peruvian Pipeline, one of the biggest engineering projects in Peruvian history. The military dictatorship of General Juan Velasco Alvarado invested around $1bn and the labour of 2,000 men in the project, which was meant to carry Peru into the first world. The usual promise.

In Nazareth, some elderly Awajún already knew about oil from times gone by. Respected for their warrior-like character – the first chroniclers called them 'head-shrinkers' – the Awajún were one of the many Amazonian nations that neither the Inca nor the Spanish soldiers could defeat. They remained isolated for hundreds of years until, in the mid-twentieth century, extractive industries and the 'apach muun', the white man, turned up with giant machines to drill into the subsoil.

Mr Cuñachí was a boy who didn't speak Spanish when the oil pipeline came along. Back then, Nazareth was a handful of wood-and-thatch huts scattered between the forest and a brown river that tumbled along a bed of enormous smooth stones. The Awajún wore brown cotton tunics and seed necklaces. They painted their faces with the red dye from achiote seeds. They took ayahuasca to communicate with the jungle spirits. For centuries, the people of the Andes knew them as 'aguarunas', from the Quechua 'awajruna', 'man who weaves'. But in their language, they have always called themselves 'liaénts': 'the true men'.

One day some engineers arrived with their families and set up a camp, ready to build a section of the pipeline. Mr Cuñachí used to play with the children of those newcomers, the white children. He swapped papayas for plastic cars, and hunting blowpipes for rubber catapults. He learnt Spanish. When construction began, military helicopters flew in every day carrying huge pieces of piping. While the adults hacked out paths with machetes to make way for the machines, the Awajún children ran around and played hide-and-seek in the uninstalled pipes. When the work finished, Williams, the US company in charge of the construction, decided to bury all the remaining material under the football pitch where Osman and his friends now play, because it was cheaper to bury it than to move it. One day, the engineers left. Then a group of families left the woodland to settle in the abandoned camp, which was infested with black ants that gobbled up rats and scared away the snakes. There they founded their first school. Then came the road, electricity, cable TV, the medical clinic, and hundreds of indigenous people and outsiders attracted by the apparent prosperity.

Almost half a century later, Nazareth is a village of fishermen, farmers, small-scale retailers and motorcycle-taxi drivers who live their lives around the Chiriaco. Right now, like any Awajún boy, Osman Cuñachí could be fishing or swimming there, but he's not allowed. Since the spill, the environmental authorities have banned those activities because of the amount of lead and cadmium in the water and the fish. Lead is a poison which, even at low levels of exposure, can affect brain development in children, cause anaemia and high blood pressure, and have irreversible effects on the central nervous system. Cadmium can damage the kidneys, bones and lungs, and cause cancer.

The Awajún say these poisonous metals come from the oil. Petroperú says that oil contains negligible amounts of these metals. Germán Velásquez, a business consultant, retired National Police commander and Petroperú's president at the time, said the metals came from the sewage and rubbish – plastic bottles, dirty disposable nappies, used batteries, motor oil – that nearby towns threw onto the banks of the Chiriaco.

'If someone there has a chance of getting some kind of financial compensation, they'll say the oil makes them cry,' I was told by Velásquez, a greying man in his fifties, one afternoon in a Lima cafe, as he arranged his lips in a half-smile beneath his thick tortoiseshell glasses. 'I've looked into it: to be poisoned by oil, you'd have to sit in a barrel of it for three or four days. I've swum in the Chiriaco and it's fine.'

The official, corporate line is optimistic. The scientific line is not.

'Anyone who says oil is harmless is lying,' Dr Fernando Osores tells me some weeks later. He's taking a break after working for ten hours straight, attending to the boys and girls in the affected communities.

Osores is an expert in environmental toxicology and tropical diseases. For twenty years, he has been treating cases of pollution caused by mines and oil and gas companies in Peru. When there's a spill, he explains, millions of hydrocarbon molecules evaporate and quickly expand in the form of poisonous gases. Breathing them in for just a few minutes is enough to cause headaches, dizziness or stomach upsets. If someone is exposed to oil without protection for several days, it's worse: skin allergies appear, irritation in the throat, breathing difficulties. Oil is a complex mixture of hundreds of hydrocarbons. Some of them, like benzene and xylene, can damage the nervous system and, over a period of years, cause cancer. Oil spilt in rivers is another problem. It breaks down into minuscule droplets, which mix with mud particles and form a sediment on the riverbed. And so the chain reaction begins: the contaminated particles feed the bacteria. The bacteria feed tiny aquatic organisms called plankton. The plankton feed the fish. The fish feed the humans. As time goes by, oil pollution becomes invisible, with no shape or smell or sound. It's incorporeal: invisible atoms. Our senses don't notice the damage it's doing.

Dr Osores sums it up in one sentence:

'We're facing a chemical disaster.'[1]

1 No technology can fully restore a habitat damaged by an oil spill. In 1989 the *Exxon Valdez*, then one of the most sophisticated oil tankers in the world, crashed into a reef in Alaska and spilt 40 million litres of oil, polluting 1,300 miles of coastline and killing thousands of animals. It's estimated that it could take a hundred years to get rid of the remaining oil. In 2002, the tanker *Prestige*, off the coast of Galicia, poured 63,000 tonnes of oil into the sea. The fishermen who took part in the clean-up developed respiratory problems. In 2010, a BP rig spilt 700 million litres of oil into the Gulf of Mexico. That ecosystem will take decades to recover, and the citizens of Florida and Alabama suffer physical harm to this day, along with depression and anxiety.

The last hundred and fifty years of global oil consumption are just the present and immediate past of a relationship as old as the pre-Hispanic myths. Oil, or petroleum – from the Latin for 'stone oil' – was discovered and used in many places and historical periods for practical, festive, religious or magical purposes. In the Americas, the substance has had at least two names with traceable origins. The Aztecs called it 'choppotli'. The second name came from the tar pits that used to exist on the north coast of Peru: the ancient Peruvians gave the name 'copé' to those stinking ponds, on the distant fringes of the desert, whose origin stretched back to an even more ancient era, the age of the giants who, legend has it, once dug those inexplicable wells. The historian Pablo Macera has written about this superstitious view of oil, as a mysterious, unknown and therefore perhaps malign substance. The ancient Peruvians called it 'the devil's dung'.

Now, several centuries and wars and scientific advances later, our reliance on oil is so extreme as to make it a frequent topic of debate among politicians and environmentalists. In 2007, during the World Energy Conference, it was announced that the earth has enough oil reserves for one or two more centuries. According to Abdallah S. Jum'ah, then president of Saudi Aramco, the biggest oil company on the planet, the world doesn't need to worry about the end of oil for a long time to come.

Despite this corporate confidence, the International Energy Agency, which monitors the earth's energy reserves, has predicted that the world will need the equivalent of six Saudi Arabias' worth of oil reserves to meet demand until 2030. Fatih Birol, an energy specialist and the agency's executive director, warns: 'We should leave oil before it leaves us.'

Peru was the trailblazer in Latin America when it came to the commercial exploitation of black gold. In 1924, when Venezuela was just starting out as an oil nation, Peru was already the regional leader. Almost a century later, Venezuela produces 1.5 million barrels per day, according to OPEC. Peru produces less than three per cent of that amount. The nationalist dream of becoming an oil giant ended in failure: today the North Peruvian Pipeline functions at just ten per cent of its capacity. The available oil – which is extracted from the Amazon, where the Awajún and other ethnic groups live, and is thicker and more expensive to refine than oil from the Middle East – is running out, but the population is growing and with it the consumption of fuel. Peru is among the twenty countries 'most addicted' to oil, according to the BP Statistical Review of World Energy. And it's the fourth most vulnerable country in America to the harm caused by global warming and the use of fossil fuels. Oil follows the same pattern as the meat industry: rich countries gain far more from consuming it than poor countries do from producing it.

It is both necessary and obvious to say that the trillion-dollar oil industry is one of the dirtiest there is. But the fact that the energy it provides has replaced human and animal traction makes it an extraordinary step forwards, one of the greatest inventions the world has ever seen. However, scientists insist that if, by the second half of the twenty-first century, countries don't swap their current energy sources for others that are less destructive to the planet, the natural world and the current economic system will most likely collapse.

The reason for this goes beyond the ecological and is determined by force of reality: the oil that sustains us is going to run out and there's nothing we can do about it.

Osman Cuñachí doesn't understand much about environmental politics and has never heard Mr Birol speak, but he does know how hard it is to clean oil off your body when you get covered in it. Not long after collecting the crude and scrubbing his skin with motorcycle fuel, Osman fainted while marching in a school parade. The teacher told his parents that the boy would often slump over his desk and sleep during lessons. For days, he had been suffering from bad headaches and dizzy spells. There was a rash all over his arms and legs which he couldn't stop scratching. Around then, the picture of him covered in petrol went viral on social media. 'The worst ecological disaster of the past decade,' people called it. Petroperú said it was sorry about what happened, but denied hiring children to do the work. That photo of Osman, however, was the evidence that plunged the company into controversy.

Two weeks after the spill, a couple of company engineers turned up at his house to see him. With Mr Cuñachí's permission, they took Osman and his aunt to a private clinic in Piura, a region on the north coast of the country and the site of the main Petroperú refinery. They tested his blood. They X-rayed him. They took him for a walk around the square, and out to eat barbecued chicken. They put him up in a hotel with a computer where he could play *Plants vs. Zombies*, one of his favourite video games. A week and a half later he returned home with some vitamins, some paracetamol tablets, cream for his spots and a certificate of health. The boy, according to the medical report, simply had anaemia.

Back in Nazareth, Osman went to find his friends, but they didn't want to play with him any more.

'How come the company's only looking after you?' one complained. 'We collected oil as well and no one's taking us anywhere. I bet they gave you money too.'

Osman was sad for several days. Then Yolanda, his

mother, gave him a few coins and he bought some sweets for his friends. That's how they made up.

Yolanda Yampis is around thirty, with waist-length black hair. She smiles every time she speaks, as if from embarrassment. Like most Awajún women, Yampis has a high-pitched, rhythmic, contagious laugh – *heheheheeeee* – as if she's singing or mimicking the song of an unknown bird. She says that in the days after the spill, various adults from Nazareth and other nearby communities left their smallholdings to work for Petroperú.

Yampis worked for them too. The school year was about to start and she needed the money. After hiring her, the Petroperú engineers dressed her up like in one of those films about radiation disasters: white plastic boiler suit, orange helmet, protective goggles, rubber boots, gloves, and a gas mask, the kind nurses use, but which didn't stop her breathing the poisonous gases the crude gave off. For a month, along with dozens of other men and women, Yampis dug out the polluted earth with a shovel. She pulled up the remains of oil-stained vegetation and stowed it in sacks. She earned almost 4,000 soles ($1,200), ten times the pension her retired husband receives. She spent it on a fridge so she can sell fizzy drinks and beer, school materials for her four children, and a tree trunk to build another room for her house. She also paid labourers to harvest the plantain from her smallholding, which is almost half a hectare in size.

'But the money's running out,' she told me, speaking softly in broken Spanish.

Yampis was standing in the communal house with the other parents, arms crossed. She was no longer laughing: now her expression was hard, her lips pursed. She watched Dr Osores nervously in the half-light as he took blood samples from Osman, her second-oldest child.

'The spill gave me an opportunity, but what's the point if you end up getting poisoned? Maybe my children are sick. Maybe I am too. We don't know.'

Since filling his bucket with oil six months before, his mother says, Osman Cuñachí has a rash on his arms and legs. His brother Omar, the third-oldest, has headaches and diarrhoea. Like them, various children in Nazareth started feeling ill after collecting the oil from the river. Following a meeting called one week after the spill, the community sent a statement to President Humala and the health minister, demanding immediate attention. It included a list of names of the children who fell ill after collecting the oil. There were more than fifty in that community alone. Petroperú donated tons of provisions and bottled water, and arranged health campaigns to look after the residents. However, by January 2017, one year after the spill, no one in this area of rainforest had a medical certificate from the state to say whether or not they had been contaminated from contact with the crude. The government never came to Nazareth or the other affected communities to carry out a thorough examination of the families' health.[2]

'It's like the authorities are waiting until ten, twenty years have passed, until people have died, before they come and see what happened,' Dr Osores told me. He was sealing the hair, blood and urine samples inside boxes of dry ice, to be flown to the laboratory in Canada that very night.

These tests would be the first attempt to assess the contamination level among the Nazareth children. As the months went by, however, the oil spill affected not only people's health, but also some people's way of thinking. Especially when the disaster, as well as spreading fear, gave them a chance to earn some money.

---

2 The Nazareth spill wasn't unique in this respect. In 2014, more than 500,000 litres of oil were spilt in the Indigenous Native Community of Cuninico, in the Urarinas district in the region of Loreto, due to a rupture in the North Peruvian Pipeline. The crude contaminated the Marañón river, which supplied the community with water and fish. From that day on, the Kukama indigenous people saw a gradual decline in their health, and suffered from respiratory and skin diseases. To clean up the spill, Petroperú used the labour of community members, including children and teenagers. They waded into the contaminated water and collected oil in buckets. In 2015, Piura's Regional Council of Labour and Employment Promotion sanctioned Petroperú for using child labour. In 2016, the state fined it more than $3m for not fully fixing the Cuninico spill.

An Awajún man who's missing his left arm guards the Petroperú camp, near the stream where the spill occurred. It's a line of blue and green tents next to a paved road leading to the centre of Chiriaco, the main town, ten minutes from Nazareth by motorcycle taxi. Inside the tents are workers consulting maps, a couple of engineers checking Excel files on their laptops, and a very young, very bored-looking doctor in heavy make-up, sweltering in front of two electric fans turned up to the max. This is the team in charge of planning the oil clean-up. Most of them are from Lima or other cities on the coast.

At the entrance, a huge red sign warns in white block capitals:

> HIRING UNDERAGE WORKERS
> IS FORBIDDEN

It's a measure the company is taking, they explain, to avoid 'rumours in the press'.

'We do things properly at Petroperú.'

The Petroperú engineer supervising the clean-up of the Chiriaco spill is a man from Lima in his fifties. He has a pointy nose and a hurried way of speaking, and every twenty minutes he reminds me not to use his name in this piece because he's afraid of losing his job. The truck we're travelling in is full of sacks of rice, beans, tins of tuna and big plastic containers of water. They're donations from the company to some schools in ten communities that relied on the contaminated river for water.

It's a hot morning, which produces a kind of humid, stifling laziness. The anonymous engineer tells me they've done all they could to return everything to how it used to be, and now the clean-up is coming to an end.

'We've given work to more than eight hundred people, on wages they'll never see again in their lives.'

Sitting beside me, Yesenia Gonzales, the engineer's assistant, says it's true and tells me all the things she's achieved while working for Petroperú. Gonzales lives in Chiriaco but was born in Piura, a city in the region of the same name on Peru's north coast from which, in recent decades, men and women have moved to the rainforest to work on smallholdings and in shops. She's twenty-four, slim from physical labour, with a smiling face and two black, watchful, shining eyes.

When the spill took place, Gonzales was living in a little rented room with her builder husband and their two girls. She was working at a juice stall and earning ten soles ($3) for twelve hours of work. One afternoon, a friend told her that Petroperú was looking for workers to clean up the spill. For ten days, she and her husband got up at dawn to go to the camp where some fifty people, locals and outsiders, were waiting for their chance.

Now, three months into working for the company, she's done everything: wading into the river to collect oil, carrying sacks of contaminated earth, cleaning rocks one by one with a high-pressure hose. Sometimes, out of curiosity, she would pick up a little oil between her fingers: she looked at its strange colour, felt its viscosity, like a piece of black chewing gum melted in the sun. And for each working day, from 7 a.m. until 6 p.m., she earns 150 soles ($46), and double on Sundays. Yesenia Gonzales makes more than a teacher in the area.

'No one pays like that around here,' she says, widening her eyes. 'I'm very grateful to Petroperú because working with oil meant I could earn that money.'

It wasn't the first time this idea of oil as a bottomless barrel of generosity had taken hold in the region. Gonzales's excitement recalls another, older excitement, from when the Peruvian rainforest was seen as the space where that promise of prosperity would be fulfilled, thanks to the resource buried deep beneath it.

The first time an oil well was drilled in the Peruvian Amazon, the front page of the newspaper *El Comercio* – later expropriated by the military government – announced, on 17 November 1971:

BATHING IN OIL

Five hundred labourers working in the Trompeteros region (in the Loreto rainforest, northern Peru) with teams from the state oil company, sang, danced and bathed in oil, overcome with joy at having made (at precisely 7:15 a.m.) a discovery of immense importance for our country's economy. All through the morning there was great celebration in Trompeteros [. . .]. Informed of the occurrence, the President of the Republic, Divisional General Juan Velasco Alvarado, telephoned to congratulate those who made the aforementioned discovery possible.

In a burst of confidence, the then president of Petroperú, Marco Fernández Baca, a general of the regime, declared: 'Peru's economic future is assured.'

The Peruvian rainforest hadn't been this in demand since the bloody rubber boom of the mid-nineteenth century. Amazonian societies had always produced everything they needed: they hunted, fished, gathered, made the earth sprout. They didn't depend on the outside world for sustenance, nor did they have access to products they didn't produce themselves. Years later, oil fever and the construction of the North Peruvian Pipeline led to a huge demand for manpower in the Peruvian rainforest. With their company wages, the indigenous people bought radios, shotguns, medicine. More than a few spent the money on beer and prostitutes. Whole native communities stopped being self-sufficient and came to depend on their earnings from the oil companies. They moved to the cities and camps in search of a better future. Some forgot their language, their customs. In the city, they thought, they could be someone.

Four decades after that oil gushed up from beneath the rainforest, as we walk through the puddled streets of Chiriaco, you can hear the sounds of a bustling town. The engines of minibuses on the lookout for passengers. The voices of girls in tight jeans selling food in the street. Pirate reggaeton CDs playing in shops with cable TV. Hymns being sung in the doorway of an evangelical church. A rhythmic banging as some shirtless workers break up stones to build a house. Babies crying in their mothers' arms while they queue outside a bank. Loudspeakers announcing every ten minutes: 'Two people needed to unload the lorry. Make your way to the Rosita grocery store.' Since the day of the spill, Chiriaco has looked like a working-class district in Lima: with more and more noise, and more and more concrete. 'Working in oil' has doubled the number of motorcycle taxis and pharmacies and food stands. Cantinas, hostels and brothels have filled up with customers. There are even workers who, over beers in a bar, joke about 'making a hole in the pipeline' so the employment doesn't dry up. The work that hundreds of locals and new arrivals have found here cleaning up the oil has put money in everyone's pockets. Or almost everyone's.

Yesenia Gonzales tells me that several of her friends have had jobs collecting oil and that it has solved their problems. One had an eye operation. Another took her daughter to Lima for heart surgery. Another, a single mother, bought an apartment in Chiclayo, one of the most populous cities on the coast, famous for its picture-perfect beaches.

'In spite of the damage, some people are happy about what happened.'

Some might see it as opportunism.

An economist would speak of 'positive externality'.

But no, Gonzales tells me: it's survival.

The midday heat bears down on everything in this patch of the Amazon rainforest. The Petroperú truck in which we're driving around town makes its final food delivery. We park on the riverbank, opposite the Awajún community of Wachapea, one of the ten the state has identified as affected by the spill. For the clean-up, as well as manual collection and extraction with motor pumps, the workers use a biodegradable product called Orange – because it smells like the fruit – which makes the remaining oil dissolve on the surface of the river, or so it seems.[3] The anonymous engineer tells me this is why the whole area we're looking at is now clean, though perhaps there are 'slight harmless stains, as if a single drop of oil had fallen into the whole river'.

On the bank of the Chiriaco, we're met by a fair-skinned woman with grey hair and a wooden crucifix around her neck. It's Rosa Villar, the head teacher at the Fe y Alegría 62 San José school, a boarding school for part-indigenous girls and the daughters of Awajún families. She asks if her pupils can swim and play in the river yet.

'Some of them do, you see,' the religious woman explains. 'Imagine – we've got more than five hundred girls. After lunch they go off and that's it. The river is their world.'

'It's not for me to say, you know that,' the engineer

3 To clean up the spill, Petroperú contracted the Finnish company Lamor, which, according to the Nazareth residents who worked on the clean-up, used chemicals to clean the river that aren't very effective, because they make the visible oil sink to the bottom and you only have to stir it up to see it float back to the clean-looking surface. In December 2017, after analysing sediment samples, the Organisation of Supervision and Environmental Assessment concluded that the use of the chemical Orange 'didn't constitute a system of degradation of the crude on the sediment, [...] and as a result, the clean-up process wasn't entirely efficient'. In February 2018, the Assessment and Environmental Control Agency was clearer when it said that the product used by Lamor 'successfully disperses the oil stains to remove them from the surfaces they stick to during the spill. However, it has no chemical properties that allow the crude to degrade, only to disperse'.

replies. 'A while ago I would have swum in the river forty times! Now, if there are still oil particles in the tree roots, what more can I do? Tip the river upside down?'[4]

The religious woman grimaces, looking worried. She says nothing. The engineer tries to convince her, with good corporate intentions. But no amount of money can repair a damaged ecosystem overnight. You'd have to wait decades and decades, experts say, for a valley polluted by a spill to recover naturally. You'd have to wait to find out how and to what extent it would affect people's health in the future. Wait and wait. Even if human lives are now shorter.

After delivering the supplies, we follow a dirt road back to the Petroperú camp. Yesenia Gonzales, the engineer's assistant, points out a huge concrete dwelling with a slanted roof.

'Look, that's my house! People say if I already have my own house at twenty-four, who knows what I'll have in the future!'

4 Despite the environmental authorities having banned swimming and fishing in the Chiriaco because it's still contaminated with poisonous metals, in March 2016, one month after the Nazareth oil spill, a Petroperú engineer called Víctor Huarcaya said in an Awajún assembly: 'You tell me the fish from the river is contaminated and can't be eaten. I'm in a position to tell you that that's not the case: you can eat the fish. The water is clean. Probably someone out there is going to say: "Listen, but there's a stone there that's a little bit blacker." That's natural.' The episode is recorded in *Petróleo, temor al veneno mortal* ('Oil, Fear of the Mortal Poison'), a 2018 documentary by the Amazonian Centre for Anthropology and Practical Application.

After working for Petroperú for four months, Gonzales and her husband built their house. Between them, they had made around 30,000 soles ($9,000). To earn that much at the juice stall at the market, she'd have had to work for ten years non-stop and save every cent. With the salary from the oil they also repaid their debts and bought a flat-screen TV, a hi-fi, a freezer and a motorcycle taxi. They bought dolls and scooters for their two daughters. Now they have their own juice shop.

When I visited her, she told me that a friend of her husband's had just told him about a spill in a section of the North Peruvian Pipeline that crosses the Uchichiangos river, the site of another Awajún community, two hours away by car. A report from the Assessment and Environmental Control Agency, the body in charge of investigating the cause of the leak, would later say that it was caused 'by third parties', who cut into it with a saw. Since she already had experience, Gonzales thought she could get work there and save enough money to finish the backyard of her house.

'People say to me: "Don't get into oil, you'll die there. Wait five years and then you'll see, you'll get sick and die!",' said Yesenia Gonzales, with her timid smile. 'I listen to them, that's all, but I'm not afraid. I'm happy. Look at me, I'm healthy, I'm not in any pain! Now I have what I've always dreamt of.'

Edith Guerrero, a bamboo enthusiast and nutrition teacher, says she'll never forget the time a Petroperú engineer tried to tell her that oil was good for her fields.

She's standing in the rain at the mouth of the Inayo stream, from where the oil poured into the Chiriaco, the river of the Awajún. Until the day of the spill, Edith Guerrero had 800 bamboo saplings here, grazing cows, very tall peach trees and laurels, and a clean stream where the Awajún also used to fish. But four months after the accident, her forty hectares of land looked like it had been destroyed by a dozen bulldozers. The tallest trees were cut down by the workers to build bridges. All her bamboo saplings were uprooted during the process of cleaning the ground. Her plan to plant rice was ruined. She had to take her cows to other fields nearby. The water from the stream, which she used for the plants and for her cattle to drink, is contaminated. Seen from above, the stream cuts through the middle of her property like a deep, oily scar.

'Indigenous people aren't the only ones affected,' complains Edith, a long-legged farmer with lively eyes, who was born in the Cajamarca mountains, as we walk together through the mud. The downpour has turned the bare land into a huge orange puddle, and our boots sink in and get stuck. 'The workers pulled up my bamboo without my permission. "Don't worry, ma'am," they said to me, "Petroperú will pay for them."'

Edith Guerrero says that despite her complaints, and unlike other farmers who did receive compensation, she still hasn't had her losses recognised by the company.

One February day, a week after the spilt oil ruined her smallholding, Guerrero went to the Petroperú camp to demand explanations. But the engineer who spoke with her claimed to know nothing about it.

'Do you also not know where they're collecting the oil from?' Edith asked sarcastically.

'From the stream,' the engineer retorted. 'And the stream belongs to the state.'

Guerrero swallowed her anger. She left the camp and got on her motorbike. When she reached her land, she yelled at all the company workers to leave. The next day she returned with her husband, very early. They blocked the road with barbed wire. When the workers arrived, Guerrero was waiting with a stick and some whip-like stinging-nettle stems. After a week, a Petroperú engineer went to see her. He insisted she sign a document in which the company committed to paying all the costs, though it didn't specify a figure or a date.

Now, on the land that's covered in puddles, there are 800 barrels full of oil from the stream, covered with blue plastic sheeting. Some men in rubber boots and orange helmets come and go, collecting what little oil is left. There's a heap of sacks full of contaminated earth and weeds. Some yellow plastic booms lie perpendicular to the current and catch the remains of the oil, which forms a greasy film on the surface of the water.

Edith Guerrero recalls that when the environmental authorities came to see the damage, they took samples of contaminated soil using special gloves. They wore masks because they said the fumes were poisonous. It wasn't the first time they had seen a case like this. Between 2011 and 2018, the last seven years in the life of the pipeline, there have been sixty-one oil and other hydrocarbon spills. Sixty per cent of them have been caused by corrosion or operational faults, and forty per cent by acts of sabotage. In 2016 alone, including the Nazareth disaster, there were fourteen, according to the Assessment and Environmental Control Agency. That year, the environment minister, Manuel Pulgar Vidal, accused Petroperú of continuing to pump oil, even though it had been forbidden from doing so until it carried out maintenance work on the system. 'The oil pipeline is obsolete,' the minister said on national television. Days later, the president of Petroperú announced his resignation, as well as a favourable reflection on his leadership: the company's turnover during the year the spills occurred was $5bn. There wasn't a single line in the report about the environmental disaster. According to the expert report from the government office that oversees the pipeline, it hasn't received full or adequate maintenance since 1998. The company says this is due to 'austerity policies', and that it wouldn't make sense to replace the whole pipeline because it would be very expensive. In a murky, stinking world like the oil industry, it's not outrageous to think that another spill will occur.

The time I went to visit her, Edith Guerrero told me that Petroperú had telephoned her to negotiate. The company needed to build a road through her farmland to remove the 800 barrels that are stored there. The natives of Yangunga, the Awajún community across the river from her land, tried to convince her to accept: building the road would provide them with jobs, they could set up a motorcycle taxi rank and even transport their plantains more quickly to sell them in the city. But Guerrero told them she wouldn't allow the road to pass through her land if Petroperú didn't pay the 70,000 soles (more than $21,000) that she's asking for to cover everything she lost.

'If not, I'm quite happy to throw the barrels into the river – maybe then those shameless fools will understand!'

'And what did the last engineer say who came to see you?' I asked her.

'"Didn't you know, ma'am, that the oil will fertilise your rice?"'

Decked out in a seed necklace and with red lines painted on his face, Tatsuya Kabutan, the Japanese ambassador to Peru, awkwardly moves to the rhythm of the drums. Surrounded by Awajún women and children in feather skirts and headdresses, Mr Kabutan – stiff and immaculate, in a white shirt and black trousers – has just arrived at Epemimu, a mountainous part of the Nazareth community on the other bank of the Chiriaco, the river contaminated by 500,000 litres of oil.

This July morning, seven months after the spill, the scorching sun hasn't stopped the festivities: the dirt road is lined with orange flowers, palm leaves, and red and white balloons for the month of national holidays. A hundred or so people – residents, civil servants, police officers – accompany Mr Kabutan and Francisco Dumler, the housing minister, to a small podium, where they will launch a building project that their institutions worked on as a team: more than a hundred bathrooms with new toilets and showers, and a network of pipes that will transport water from a stream to each of the 180 families who live here. Comparisons with the city are inevitable: now the locals will no longer have to walk long distances to collect water in buckets or plastic bottles. Now all they have to do in order to drink water, wash their clothes or take a shower is turn on the tap.

'When this government came to power, only one in

three Peruvians in native communities or rural areas had access to drinking water,' housing minister Dumler announces from the podium. He's a robust man from Lima with a high forehead and a neat moustache. His voice booms out of some scratchy loudspeakers. 'Now we're ending the year at two in three!'

Applause and more applause. Minutes later, they come down to cut the red-and-white ribbon: the formal opening. Then, along with some children, the minister sips the potable water from the new tap. 'Delicious,' he says. Ambassador Kabutan, standing next to him, dries the sweat on his face with a handkerchief. He looks at the minister, but doesn't drink. He smiles, at least, for the official photo. Applause and more applause, please.

When the event is over I ask the minister about the contaminated river, if he knows when it will usable again. 'Let me have a word with the health minister. I'll pass your concerns on to him,' he replies as he walks past, and one of his bodyguards directs him to his 4x4, where Mr Kabutan is waiting. The head of PR – a woman with dyed-blonde hair, sunglasses and black boots – records my details on her iPhone, which has a Starbucks-themed case. Before she goes, she promises to send me her boss's response via WhatsApp. It never arrives.

The nurse Janet Tuyas, who was watching the ceremony from the side of the dirt road, sheltered from the sun by her parasol, later tells me that 'it's all just box-ticking'. She doesn't trust government projects. Tuyas is an Awajún woman with almond-shaped eyes and an athletic build, who works in the Nazareth health centre. She's lived here since she was a teenager, and it worries her that people still don't know when they will be able to use the river again.

'We can have all this, water, plumbing, but our river is practically dead,' the nurse says sadly. 'For months nobody's swum there or fished there . . . Well, almost nobody.'

Tuyas takes a planner out of her rucksack to confirm the details: a couple of months after the oil spill, she saw thirty-five patients with fever, respiratory problems, swollen tonsils, tickly throats, lumps under the skin and fungal infections. She also saw twenty-three girls whose bodies were covered in red spots like mosquito bites. Almost all of them admitted to going in the river and eating fish from it.

This afternoon, Janet Tuyas has to do her round of baby and child vaccinations. We take a motorcycle taxi that rattles up a steep, rocky dirt road. As we travel further up the mountain, every so often, among the huts and trees, we see groups of three or four barefoot children, in dusty clothes, playing with sticks or balls or plastic bottles. Some of them point when they see me – apach muun, apach muun! – and laugh. Sometimes the community seems to be entirely populated by children, or by young girls holding children by the hand, or with babies in their arms or tied to their backs with a shawl, as if they were wearing a rucksack. In the Peruvian rainforest, three in ten girls get pregnant or have a child before they're old enough to get their ID.

'I wanted something different,' says Tuyas, who's thirty-nine and has no children herself. 'But not all women have that option.'

In Nazareth, she tells me, the Awajún men refuse to use condoms, and they don't let their partners use contraception either. They say they don't want their wives to be unfaithful to them. 'We don't need that stuff from you,' they joke when the nurse insists. 'We know how to take care of them.' Although, Tuyas says, there's an even more serious problem: since the day of the spill, as well as an increase in diseases like dermatitis, fevers and diarrhoea, there has also been a rise in cases of HIV.

Amazonas, the region where Nazareth is located, has the highest number of indigenous people infected with the virus: according to statistics from the Ministry of Health, the figure leapt from thirty-five reported cases in 2011 to 244 in 2017. Of those, forty-six were adolescent girls. Tuyas says that, as well as a lack of information, this is due to the fact that many men, now they have more money in their pockets, are going to cantinas and brothels in the city or nearby towns. They get infected there, and then come back and infect their wives. The situation is made worse by the fact that some men who are infected don't trust the science: they're not sick, they swear; they're victims of witchcraft.

When one of Tuyas's colleagues, a nurse from Lima, gave one couple the diagnosis, they didn't accept the antiretroviral treatment and instead threatened to kill him: they thought he was a wizard who had 'done them harm'. The nurse had to request a transfer to another health centre. Because of that, Tuyas says, they're now very careful how they explain it. As a precaution, they protect the patients' identity using code names.

The nurses call them 'Code White'.

The Awajún call them 'jata susamu', 'the bewitched'.

Like viruses, which attack invisibly, the problems oil leaves behind are impossible to see. 'It's like something's got into the land, the water, the air,' says Tuyas. Some elderly Awajún, she tells me, believe it's 'an evil spirit'. They've seen them in their ayahuasca visions: black beings that move around on the surface of the water like oily stains.

'In the Amazonian cosmovision, the oil spirit has always existed,' the Italian anthropologist Emanuele Fabiano explained to me. He spent six years living with the Urarina nation in the rainforest around the Corrientes river, in northern Peru, to study the impact of the spills on those villages. 'These spirits were "good neighbours" when nobody disturbed them. But the oil companies' activities and the spills have woken them up, made them angry and drawn them out of their traditional territories. Now they live in the communities.'

The Urarina – who, like the Awajún, have been used as cheap labour to clean up the leaks in the North Peruvian Pipeline – say the oil spirit curls up inside people's bodies like a snake. If you work cleaning the fuel from the river, it will follow you home. Then it will infect your wife and children, they will break out in spots, their heads will ache, they'll struggle to breathe. Eventually you'll stop wanting to work, or spend time with your family. Maybe you'll have money – the Urarina warn – but the sadness will make you ill.

In Nazareth, our motorcycle-taxi driver, Asterio Pujupat, who has nine children and refuses to use contraception, told me later that he knows various local people like that, and that it's easy to tell which ones have taken the Petroperú wage. Opposite his palm-thatched bamboo hut, he points out a house three times the size, with two storeys, made of new planks of wood and corrugated iron. A small cable TV aerial sits on one side of the roof. 'That man worked in oil,' said Asterio, in the little Spanish he knows. He was disappointed not to get a job in the clean-up himself because he'd lost his ID. Meanwhile, other Awajún he met as the days went by – some sixty adults from

Nazareth were hired by Petroperú – had better luck. Or perhaps not.

'Now my children are going to school in the town. And I'm building my house, I've already bought the bricks,' says Américo Taijín, a builder, who spent three months cleaning the stream with pressure hoses.

'Before I just did odd jobs, then suddenly the spill happened and it gave us opportunities. If I get sick later on, who knows,' says Abel Wanputsang, a welder, who opened a bar with disco lights, a sound system and a fridge for selling beer.

'God is great because we were suffering here, we didn't have any work. The cacao plants weren't growing well and neither was the plantain,' recalls Nino Cuñachí, a farmer, who used what he earned to set up a clothes shop in his house. He brought the clothes back from Gamarra, a textiles market in Lima.

'I wouldn't call it an opportunity, the work's not good for you. I told my son not to go, but he didn't listen,' says Salomón Awanansh, an Awajún leader and fan of Che Guevara. His son now has a motorcycle taxi, a fridge and a 36-inch flat-screen TV.

'We cleaned up the oil with a special product, but my teachers say the crude has just settled in the river. I stopped because I was feeling dizzy, weak,' says Lenin Taijín, a fifth-year environmental engineering student, who used the money to pay his university fees and finish building a room for his future child.

'The spill gave us work, but now I want a medical test, I want to know if there's anything wrong with me. I saw two of my friends faint,' says a worried Leonardo Pujupat, a plantain farmer, who bought seeds and a chainsaw, painted his house blue and gave it a corrugated iron roof.

'My partner was out of work but now he earns good money,' says the nurse, Janet Tuyas, as we travel down the road, working through her round. 'Now we've built a little house. The problem is that he had to go there and get covered in the stuff.'

When her husband came back from collecting oil in the river, Tuyas saw that the protective suit he'd been given by Petroperú was useless: all his clothes were stained black. And so, to avoid getting his clothes dirty, he started wearing just underpants with the suit. He came home every night reeking of fuel. Tuyas says that now her husband wants to go and clean up another spill, in Morona, in the Loreto region of the rainforest, a few days away by boat. Some 300,000 litres of oil contaminated the valley there after part of the pipeline wore away. Her husband wants to earn more money so they can put doors and windows on their house.

'I just hope he doesn't have anything genetic after spending all day in the oil,' sighs the nurse, who hasn't given up on wanting to be a mother in a few years' time. 'Imagine – what if my child is born with a disease?'

After 6 p.m., the torches on our phones barely give off enough light for us to avoid the puddles on the footpath. Janet Tuyas and I visit a few more families, and then we come to the final house: the house of a Code White.

Inside the thatched wooden hut, a pair of candles in a corner provide the only light, casting our oversized shadows on the earthen floor. There's a log stove. A rusty shelf of plates and pans. A bag of pills on a red plastic table. A wooden platform with a mattress on top, and on the mattress a girl. A white net curtain hangs between us and her and protects her from the mosquitoes. A newborn baby sleeps at her chest. Two women, her neighbours, are looking after her, and they talk in Awajún with the nurse. In the half-light, you can just about see the girl's face, the dark shadows under her eyes, and her thin body. Her voice is a whisper. She gave birth five days ago, Tuyas tells me. She's seventeen. She asks me not to include her name.

Before we arrived, the nurse told me about her situation. Her husband, an Awajún, worked cleaning oil from the river, got her pregnant and infected her. He then disappeared once he'd received his Petroperú wages. The young woman's friends swear he went off to the city with another woman. Tuyas tells the mother not to breastfeed the child so that she doesn't infect him. But after speaking to her in Awajún for a few minutes, the nurse looks downcast.

'She's already breastfed the baby,' she translates for me. 'She says she's got nothing else to give him.'

That night, as we were walking back to the health centre so that she could drop off her rucksack of vaccines, Janet Tuyas thought about possible ways of helping her people. A lot of things changed after the oil spill, some for the better, but the underlying problems have only got worse. In the Nazareth rainforest, many families' precarity and the indifference of the state means that even the ways of loving and surviving have changed.

The last time I saw her, Tuyas told me that sometimes, when she was visiting Awajún mothers and grand-mothers, they served her roast boquichico or catfish that they'd caught in the Chiriaco, the contaminated river. Not wanting to be rude, the nurse lied and promised to eat the fish at home, but really she threw it away. At first, she begged them to wait until the river was clean again, but one of them got annoyed and said: 'Well, what are we supposed to eat if we don't have any money?' Ever since then, Janet Tuyas the nurse, who doesn't earn much but enough to buy fish in town, has decided to keep quiet.

The Chiriaco is a sprawling highway of mud-coloured water. It's worrying that on this sunny September Sunday, eight months after the oil spill, some community members are fishing here, and that it's possible for fish to live here, in this polluted water. People wash clothes and swim in the river, over the full ten kilometres of its length. The Chiriaco winds its way imperturbably along, and on its surface are canoes, some stained black, and bits of wood, plastic bags, and now and then the body of a small dead animal.

Osman Cuñachí, the Awajún boy, looks at the river and admits that he misses it, but says that ever since the day of the spill he hasn't dared swim there. At first glance, there's no sign of oil in the water. But until the environmental authorities say so officially, his dad has told him he's not allowed. Or else.

'Some people eat the fish because there's nowhere else to get food. In my house we don't eat it, even if people give it to us. Now I have to eat more vegetables, and I don't like them.'

Eating more vegetables, says Osman, is one of many pieces of advice the doctor gave his mum this morning, after explaining what was happening in his skinny eleven-year-old body because he'd had contact with the crude.

As promised, Dr Fernando Osores came back to Nazareth with a delegation from the National Co-ordinator for Human Rights and the Amazonian Centre for

159

Anthropology and Practical Application, to pass on the results of the tests analysed in Québec: those blood, urine and hair samples from twenty-five boys and girls who collected oil in the river.

The lab tests confirmed what Osores, an expert in this kind of disaster, suspected: the children tested had cadmium, lead, arsenic and mercury in their organisms. In an assembly exclusively for Awajún families, Osores explained the situation: normally no human being would have even a single particle of those poisonous metals in their bloodstream, but the results show that these children have more than the World Health Organisation limit.

'Now the state has to monitor them closely and decide if our finding is a one-off or persistent exposure,' Osores said to me later. 'If it's persistent, then these people are poisoning themselves.'

If the doctor's hypothesis is proved correct, by the time they're teenagers, in maybe five or ten years, these children – especially those weakened by anaemia and malnutrition – could suffer damage to their nervous system and learning ability, and develop high blood pressure, kidney failure and even cancer when they reach adulthood. Faced with that possibility, the state should assess the danger and take immediate action. But as the months go by, it seems that little or nothing will be done to deal with the emergency.

While that was going on in Nazareth, more than 1,000

kilometres away, at the company headquarters – a brutalist building shaped like an oil rig in the financial centre of Lima – the heads of Petroperú were just beginning their attempts to explain themselves to the press. Through official statements, the company declared that of the fourteen spills in the Amazon in 2016 – the highest number in the past decade – nine were the result of third-party sabotage. They insinuated that greedy locals were to blame for sawing holes in the pipeline. But a committee from the Congress of the Republic, which investigated the spills in 2017, concluded, among other things, that there were no signs that could reasonably suggest the spills were caused by local communities. On the contrary, there was evidence of 'possible crimes and instances of corruption or at least an unacceptable lack of training among Petroperú staff'. The final report – sent on to the public prosecutor's office for investigation – recognised that the root of the problem was the pipeline's lack of maintenance. And it added this piece of information: in the last nine years, that steel serpent had spilt at least four million litres of oil into the Amazon. Two Olympic swimming pools' worth had been upended into the rivers and valleys where thousands of families like the Awajún live.

It's a perverse paradox of development that something as horrific as an oil spill and the death of a river could temporarily benefit a town. This is a reality that tends not to appear in the news, that short circuits our brains, that makes us confront our contradictions. The story of Nazareth – home to Osman Cuñachí and 'the oil children' – is just one small mirror in which we see ourselves reflected.

As we leave the Chiriaco behind and return to his hut, Osman tells me the doctor spoke to his mother and now she's very worried. He didn't really understand what the doctor said, and in fact, nor did his mother. Osman just understands that he has 'something, a disease', and that for now he doesn't feel ill.

'And what did you tell your mum?' I ask him.

'If I have a disease and die, well, then I die,' Osman smiles, before going off to play with his friends.

The idea of death still seems a long way away to him.

That's how it should be.

The last time we spoke, in February 2017, one year after the spill, Osman Cuñachí had just turned twelve. From his dad's mobile phone, he told me he'd started his first year of secondary school. He was still getting up at five in the morning to ride to school on his bicycle. He would come back at one in the afternoon to have lunch, play with his dogs, Lucky, Bobby and Micky, do his homework, help his mum in the smallholding, watch *Dragon Ball Z* with his siblings, and catch scorpions with his friends. He wasn't feeling dizzy as often, and only small scars were left on his arms and legs after all the scratching. 'I just want to be healthy, like a normal kid, and not be scared of getting a tumour one day,' he said. He still wants to move to Lima eventually and pursue his plans: become an architect or professional goalkeeper. Learn karate. Swim in the sea. Go to the cinema. Be less shy with girls. Finally have his own smartphone.

He's twelve years old.

He has, he should have, his whole life ahead of him.

EPILOGUE

EPILOGUE

'It is in writing it down that I now understand.'

J. M. G. Le Clézio
'The African'

I'd like to say it began differently, but I can't: the seeds of this book were sown by chance. These are not stories I initially chose to write. Instead, they are the product of challenges I was set by my editors, but which now, in hindsight, seem to have been leading somewhere all along. It was around the winter of 2012 when I began publishing long-form journalism in the pages of *Etiqueta Verde*, at a rate of one piece per year, about indigenous communities in the Peruvian Andes and Amazon. Stories of men and women who take on economic and political power, mafias and corruption, to defend the forest, mountains and rivers they call home. Stories about realities which those of us who work as journalists in cities are often oblivious to or disregard, and when we do dare to look at them, and write about them, we tend to misinterpret the codes, romanticise the poverty, and even demonise the demands.

This was how, in the five years that followed – as well as

the stories I tell here – I came to publish reportage and profiles in different magazines and co-authored books. I wrote about an engineer from the Peruvian rainforest who travels between Mexico and India to take on the garbage mafias; a cartographer who teaches the Harakbut indigenous people how to use flying robots to protect their forests from illegal mining; a farmer and huayno violinist who fights climate change in order to save 300 potato species from extinction; an Asháninka leader who unites her people to denounce the state and prevent a reservoir from being built on ancestral land.

At the time, when people asked why I was spending month after month researching and writing about these things, I didn't have a clear answer, just an intuition. And then at the end of 2015, when I quit my job to do a master's degree in Spain and revisited those articles, I realised they contained more than journalistic accusations: a hidden thread ran through them all, more complex even than the environmental subject matter.

With time and travel and reading, I came to understand that when I wrote about those land disputes, and about the people who inhabit and defend the mountains and jungles, I wasn't 'giving them a voice'. I was giving a voice to myself. I had been writing, without meaning to, about the place my family came from.

*

I was born in Lima, but I grew up in a household with Amazonian roots. My maternal grandmother, Mamita Lilí, was born in Vistoso, a community of people from the Kukama Kukamiria indigenous nation in Peru's northern rainforest, which was destroyed in the 1940s when a river burst its banks. At the age of thirteen, with three years of primary education under her belt, my grandmother decided to move to Lima, to the house of an aunt who promised to educate her. She wanted to become a nurse, but, as happens with thousands of girls from the provinces in my country, she ended up being exploited: her aunt made her work as a maid, and then, to get rid of her, married her off to a neighbour ten years her senior. He promised to take her back to the rainforest, to 'her land', if she agreed to be his wife. Mamita Lilí was fourteen. My grandfather, an electrician from Celendín, in the mountains of Cajamarca, didn't keep his word.

Over time, while living in a neighbourhood in the San Martín de Porres district in the north of Lima, Mamita Lilí raised eight children and built a family home thanks to her work as a seamstress for the Peruvian air force. Because she was pretty and nice, she told me, she used to be invited to official dinners. There, she began to copy the elegant manners of the military wives. She learnt to use a knife and fork, to drink cocktails instead of fizzy drinks, to sit with her legs crossed, to wear make-up.

Little by little, she adapted the cadence of her speech to match the way people spoke in Lima. She took up betting on horses and playing the lottery. She managed to send almost all her children to university. In a city that even today sees the Amazon and the Andes as a land of exotic, impoverished people, only by becoming more 'Liman' did Mamita Lilí believe she could get ahead. Getting ahead in the city meant, in a sense, ceasing to be who she was.

I decided to explore this family history after making all these trips to the interior of Peru and writing the texts that form this book. Just like my grandmother, the central figures in these stories are conflicted about what defines them, and work to untangle these conflicts. Their lives do not, in the words of Svetlana Alexievich, 'migrate into history'; rather, they 'disappear without a trace'. The difference is that most of them didn't move to the city to get ahead, as Mamita Lilí did. They opted to stay and wage a kind of war – inside and outside themselves – to stop their culture and the life they know being crushed by the might of a corporation, mafia or government that treats them as if they aren't citizens.

They wage wars that no one officially calls wars. Wars over land and identity. Wars between clashing visions of progress. Wars that have been going on for generations in the communities of Latin America, like a heavy, silent inheritance that has been passed down to us and we cannot easily give back.

In Peru, seven in ten social conflicts are caused by the exploitation of natural resources. The timber, gold and oil industries were central to the different modernisation projects in Latin American countries – whether the governments were left or right wing, authoritarian or democratic – but at the same time they have led to crimes being inflicted on indigenous people and rural communities, crimes that we have ignored or normalised because they happen so frequently.

In Latin America – the most urbanised and at the same time the most unequal region in the world – the idea of modernity has often involved a monocultural and aggressive vision of history. In this book, wood, gold and oil are not only materials: they are metaphors which speak of the human conflicts caused by opposing views of development. These conflicts reveal the contradictions at play in our societies, and the conspiracy of apathy and cynicism that governs our everyday lives, but also the extraordinary feats we are capable of when we feel that something that defines us is under attack.

The word 'interior', in that sense, does not refer only to a physical space – the interior of the earth from which natural resources are extracted; the interior of the country, the 'Perú profundo' described by José María Arguedas, where these conflicts take place. It also suggests the mental and emotional space of human needs and desires, such as shelter, ostentation, power, and the drive to overcome. I chose wood, gold and oil as symbols of progress, that panacea which everyone pursues. The question is what we are prepared to sacrifice, as individuals and as a society, to achieve it.

I have tried to sketch out a few answers by investigating, not the events of the social conflicts, but rather the human questions at their heart. I am interested in the pressure that events can exert on people, and in recording – in the words of Julio Ramón Ribeyro – 'the psychological history of a human decision'.

What makes a woman decide to risk her and her children's lives and spend years fighting a mining company that wants to evict her from some land? What makes an electrician decide to leave his wife, his children and the comforts of the city to go into the depths of the rainforest, become an indigenous leader and face death at the hands of illegal loggers? What makes a child decide to wade into a river contaminated by oil – a disaster that, instead of being a calamity for his village, suddenly becomes an unexpected source of progress? What interests lie behind these decisions? To what extent do they change someone's life forever, and the lives of the people around them?

The possible answers lie in the stories themselves, and are different in each case: anger, fear, threatened dignity, ambition, loneliness, death. They all combine or act individually upon us.

The true social and environmental conflicts don't happen out there, at the roadblocks and mass demonstrations. They happen deep within us first, in what some call the soul and others the subconscious. And when they do happen, we have a sense, explicit or not, that something that belongs to us and defines us has been fractured, perhaps beyond repair.

That world, considered by the 'dominant culture' to be 'marginal', 'backward', 'not modern', is not a separate territory which I have visited, as many journalists do, in order to report on it. The world I depict here is the world I come from.

In September 2016, on a day like any other, I made my first visit with Mamita Lilí to Pucallpa, the rainforest of her childhood, in an attempt to retrace her origins. I wanted to know the woman she ceased to be when she moved to the capital city. I recorded hours and hours of conversations. I interviewed her cousins, brothers and uncles, who – incredibly – were still alive. At the end of the trip, days before I moved to Barcelona, we vowed to go back again soon, that time to visit the rainforest where Vistoso once was. We wanted to know what was left of the vanished community where she was born. She also gave me a white envelope containing old photos, personal correspondence, her birth certificate: fragments of memory. That was the last time I saw her. Two months later, when I was beginning to organise my ideas for this book, Mamita Lilí died of cancer. She was seventy-eight.

Now, writing these lines, I think about what has led me to this point, to this page. I remember how I felt as my grandmother was telling me about her life, how internal connections suddenly appeared that bound her story to my own, and to my work as a reporter. From that day on, this project began to take shape within me in a different way, as if a jigsaw puzzle I'd tipped onto a table were solving itself with no help from my hands. I'm pleased it arose and developed that way. The stories I have told here contain places, details and contradictions that I identify with and still feel drawn to. Writing this book has been a way of opening the door to them.

San Martín de Porres, Lima, September 2018

BIBLIOGRAPHY

I have tried not to obstruct the reading experience with bibliographical references, but I have also been careful with my information. The quotations and facts included in this book are taken from the works listed below. Although these works are not cited explicitly in the text, reading them has played a vital role in the work of understanding and exploring the stories in this book.

Wood

Adario, Paulo, et al., *Deadly Environment: The Dramatic Rise in Killings of Environmental and Land Defenders* (Lima: Global Witness, November 2014).

Amazonian Centre for Anthropology and Practical Application & International Work Group for Indigenous Affairs, *Libro Azul británico. Informes de Roger Casement y otras cartas sobre las atrocidades en el Putumayo* ('British

Blue Book: Roger Casement's Reports and Other Letters About the Atrocities in the Putumayo') (Lima: Amazonian Centre for Anthropology and Practical Application & International Work Group for Indigenous Affairs, December 2011).

Calvo, César, *The Three Halves of Ino Moxo: Teachings of the Wizard of the Upper Amazon*, trans. Kenneth Symington (Rochester: Inner Traditions, 1995).

Everett, Daniel L., *Don't Sleep, There Are Snakes: Life and Language in the Amazonian Jungle* (London: Profile, 2008).

Fowles, John, *The Tree* (London: Aurum Press, 1979).

Global Witness, *At What Cost? Irresponsible Business and the Murder of Land and Environmental Defenders in 2017* (London: Global Witness, July 2018).

Goncalves, Marilyne Pereira, et al., *Justice for Forests: Improving Criminal Justice Efforts to Combat Illegal Logging* (Washington, DC: World Bank, 2012).

Grann, David, *The Lost City of Z: A Legendary British Explorer's Deadly Quest to Uncover the Secrets of the Amazon* (London: Simon & Schuster, 2017).

Harley, J. B., *The New Nature of Maps: Essays in the History of Cartography*, ed. Paul Laxton (Baltimore: Johns Hopkins University Press, 2001).

Jahren, Hope, *Lab Girl* (London: Fleet, 2016).

Mancuso, Stefano, and Alessandra Viola, *Brilliant Green:*

The Surprising History and Science of Plant Intelligence, trans. Joan Benham (Washington, DC: Island Press, 2015).

Mytting, Lars, *Norwegian Wood: Chopping, Stacking, and Drying Wood the Scandinavian Way*, trans. Robert Ferguson (London: MacLehose Press, 2015).

Neuman, William, and Andrea Zárate, 'Corruption in Peru Aids Cutting of Rain Forest', *New York Times*, 18 October 2013.

Notess, Laura, et al., *The Scramble for Land Rights: Reducing Inequity between Communities and Companies* (Washington, DC: World Resources Institute, July 2018).

Osorio, Leonardo, *Landscape Appropriation and Socioenvironmental Adaptability of Ashéninka People in the Border Area of Amazonian Peru and Brazil* (Canterbury: University of Kent School of Anthropology and Conservation, 2012).

Palumbo, Ornella, 'Un bosque de problemas' ('A Forest of Problems'), *Hildebrandt en sus trece*, Lima, 3–9 October issue, 2014.

Pollan, Michael, *The Botany of Desire: A Plant's-Eye View of the World* (London: Bloomsbury, 2002).

Poméon, Alexandra, et al., *Steadfast in Protest: Annual Report* (Paris: Observatory for the Protection of Human Rights Defenders, 2011).

Santos Granero, Fernando, and Frederica Barclay, eds, *Guía*

Etnográfica de la Alta Amazonía (Volumen V) ('Ethnographic Guide to the High Amazon, Volume V) (Lima: Smithsonian Tropical Research Institute & French Institute of Andean Studies, 2005).

Urrunaga, Julia, 'Un concierto de rock por los árboles. ¿A qué suena una guitarra hecha con madera ilegal?' ('A Rock Concert from the Trees: What Does a Guitar Made of Illegal Wood Sound Like?'), *Etiqueta Verde*, no. 6, October 2012.

Urrunaga, Julia, and Andrea Johnson, *The Laundering Machine: How Fraud and Corruption in Peru's Concession System are Destroying the Future of its Forests* (Washington, DC: Environmental Investigation Agency, 2012).

Urrunaga, Julia, and Andrea Johnson, *Moment of Truth: Promise or Peril for the Amazon as Peru Confronts its Illegal Timber Trade* (Washington, DC: Environmental Investigation Agency, January 2018).

Varese, Stefano, *Salt of the Mountain: Campa Asháninka History and Resistance in the Peruvian Jungle*, trans. Susan Giersbach Rascón (Norman, OK: University of Oklahoma Press, 2002).

Wallace, Scott, 'Mahogany's Last Stand', *National Geographic*, vol. 32, no. 4, April 2013.

Gold

Anaya, James, *Report A/HRC/24/41, Extractive Industries and Indigenous Peoples: Report of the Special Rapporteur on the Rights of Indigenous Peoples*, United Nations General Assembly, 1 July 2013.

Angier, Natalie, 'Moonlighting as a Conjurer of Chemicals', *New York Times*, 12 October 2010.

Barenys, Marta, et al., 'Heavy Metal and Metalloids Intake Risk Assessment in the Diet of a Rural Population Living Near a Gold Mine in the Peruvian Andes (Cajamarca)', *Food Chemical Toxicology Journal*, vol. 71, September 2014.

Bernstein, Peter L., *The Power of Gold: The History of an Obsession* (Chichester: John Wiley, 2001).

Berthelot, Marcelin, *Les origines de l'alchimie* (Paris: Steinheil, 1885).

Calderón, Fernando, ed., *La protesta social en América Latina* ('Social Protest in Latin America') (Buenos Aires: Siglo XXI, 2012).

Costa Aponte, Francisco et al., *Evolución de la pobreza monetaria 2007–2017. Informe técnico* ('Evolution of Monetary Poverty 2007–17: Technical Report') (Lima: National Institute of Statistics and Informatics, April 2018).

De Echave, José, and Alejandro Diez, *Más allá de Conga* ('Beyond Conga') (Lima: Peruvian Network for Sustainable Globalisation, 2013).

Diamond, Jared, *Guns, Germs and Steel: A Short History of Everybody for the Last 13,000 Years* (London: Chatto & Windus, 1997).

Galeano, Eduardo, *The Open Veins of Latin America: Five Centuries of the Pillage of a Continent*, trans. Cedric Belfrage (New York: Monthly Review Press, 1971).

Harari, Yuval Noah, *Sapiens: A Brief History of Humankind* (London: Harvill Secker, 2014).

Knight Piésold Consultores, *Minera Yanacocha S. R. L. Proyecto Conga: Estudio de impacto ambiental – Informe final* ('Yanacocha Mining Company S.R.L. Conga Project: Environmental Impact Study – Final Report') (Lima: Knight Piésold Consultores, February 2010).

Larmer, Brook, 'The Real Price of Gold', *National Geographic*, January 2009.

Lino Cornejo, Elizabeth, *Josefina. La mujer en la lucha por la tierra* ('Josefina: The Woman in the Fight for Land') (Lima: Pakarina Ediciones, 2014).

Lips, Ferdinand, *Gold Wars: The Battle Against Sound Money as Seen From a Swiss Perspective* (New York: Foundation for the Advancement of Monetary Education, 2002).

Mann, Charles C., *1491: New Revelations of the Americas Before Columbus*, new edn (London: Granta, 2006).

—, *1493: How Europe's Discovery of the Americas Revolutionized Trade, Ecology and Life on Earth* (London: Granta, 2011).

Mayer, Enrique, *Ugly Stories of the Peruvian Agrarian Reform* (Durham: Duke University Press, 2009).

More, Thomas, *Utopia* (Cambridge: CUP, 2002).

National Co-ordinator for Human Rights, *Informe anual. Un año del gobierno de Ollanta Humala* (2011–2012) ('Annual Report: A Year of the Ollanta Humala Government, 2011–2012') (Lima: National Co-ordinator for Human Rights, 2012).

Oxfam America, *Geographies of Conflict: Mapping Overlaps Between Extractive Industries and Agricultural Land Uses in Ghana and Peru*, March 2014.

Perlez, Jane, and Lowell Bergman, 'Tangled Strands in Fight Over Peru Gold Mine', *New York Times*, 25 October 2005.

Public Prosecutor's Office, Lima, *Reporte mensual de conflictos sociales No 173* ('Monthly Report of Social Conflicts No. 173') (Lima: Public Prosecutor's Office, July 2018).

Rostworowski, María, *History of the Inca Realm*, trans. Harry B. Iceland (Cambridge: CUP, 1999).

Scorza, Manuel, *Drums for Rancas*, trans. Edith Grossman (London: Secker and Warburg, 1977).

Todorov, Tzvetan, *The Conquest of America: The Question of the Other*, trans. Richard Howard (New York: Harper & Row, 1984).

Virilio, Paul, *The Administration of Fear*, trans. Ames Hodges (London: Semiotext(e), 2012).

Wiener, Raúl, and Juan Torres, *Large-Scale Mining: Do They Pay the Taxes They Should? The Yanacocha Case* (Lima: LATINDADD, 2014).

World Gold Council, Goldhub/Gold Demand Trends (www.gold.org/research/gold-demand-trends).

Yacoub, Cristina, et al., 'Trace Metal Content of Sediments Close to Mine Sites in the Andean Region', *The Scientific World Journal*, vol. 2012, April 2012.

Oil

Beavan, Colin, *No Impact Man: Saving the Planet One Family at a Time* (London: Piatkus, 2009).

Descola, Philippe, *The Spears of Twilight: Life and Death in the Amazon Jungle*, trans. Janet Lloyd (London: HarperCollins, 1996).

Guallart, José María. *Entre pongo y cordillera. Historia de la etnia Aguaruna-Huambisa* ('Between Gorge and Mountain Range: History of the Aguaruna-Huambisa Ethnic Group') (Lima: Amazonian Centre for Anthropology and Practical Application, 1990).

Guerra, Margarita, et al., *Historia del petróleo en el Perú*

('History of Oil in Peru') (Lima: Petróleos del Perú, 2008).

Heinberg, Richard, *The Party's Over: Oil, War and the Fate of Industrial Societies* (Forest Row, East Sussex: Clairview, 2003).

Herzog, Werner, *Conquest of the Useless: Reflections from the Making of* Fitzcarraldo, trans. Krishna Winston (New York: Ecco, 2009).

Jochamowitz, Luis, *Crónicas del petróleo en el Perú* ('Chronicles of Oil in Peru') (Lima: Grupo Repsol YPF, 2001).

Kapuściński, Ryszard, *Shah of Shahs*, trans. Christopher de Bellaigue (London: Penguin, 2006).

Klare, Michael T., *Rising Powers, Shrinking Planet: The New Geopolitics of Energy* (London: Oneworld, 2008).

Leonard, Annie, *The Story of Stuff: How Our Obsession with Stuff is Trashing the Planet, Our Communities, and our Health – and a Vision for Change* (New York: Free Press, 2010).

Macera, Pablo, *Historia del petróleo peruano (Volumen I). Las breas coloniales del siglo XVIII* ('History of Peruvian Oil, Volume I: The Colonial Tar Pits of the Eighteenth Century') (Lima: National University of San Marcos, 1963).

Paun, Ashim, et al., *Fragile Planet: Scoring Climate Risks Around the World* (London: HSBC Global Research, March 2018).

Rifkin, Jeremy, *The Hydrogen Economy: The Creation of the Worldwide Energy Web and the Redistribution of Power on Earth* (Oxford: Polity, 2002).

Rosell, Juan, *¿Y después del petróleo, qué? Luces y sombras del futuro energético mundial* ('And After Oil, What? Lights and Shadows of the Future of World Energy') (Barcelona: Deusto, 2007).

Ruiz, Juan Carlos, and Álvaro Másquez, *Derecho desde los márgenes. Pueblos indígenas y litigio constitucional estratégico en el Perú* ('Law from the Margins: Indigenous Peoples and Strategic Constitutional Litigation in Peru') (Lima: Legal Defence Institute, April 2018).

Shah, Sonia, *Crude: The Story of Oil* (New York: Seven Stories, 2005).

Tierney, Patrick, *Darkness in El Dorado: How Scientists and Journalists Devastated the Amazon* (New York: Norton, 2000).

ACKNOWLEDGEMENTS

A book never depends solely on the work of its author. And this one, though short, exists thanks to the help of many people.

I would like to thank the people who, over the many journeys I made for this book, trusted me with their testimony: above all Edwin Chota's siblings and his Asháninka relatives in Saweto; Máxima Acuña and her children; and Osman Cuñachí, his parents and the Awajún community of Nazareth. I hope I have done my best to describe the battles you go on fighting to this day.

Thank you to Jerónimo Pimentel for believing in this project from the start and waiting with zen-like patience until the very end.

To Elda Cantú, the editor of these pages, whose intelligence and generosity pushed me to finish what I had been putting off for too long.

To Julio Villanueva Chang and Eliezer Budasoff, brothers/editors/teachers who, during all-nighters at *Etiqueta Negra*, read, critiqued and took a scalpel to the earliest versions of these articles.

To Jorge Carrión, my supervisor on the MA in Creative Writing at the Pompeu Fabra University, and to Leonardo Faccio, my deadline buddy. During my year in Barcelona, they both made me feel welcome and helped me to think, think and think through this project.

To Martín Caparrós, for his meticulous advice in the Journalism Books Workshop at the FNPI in Oaxaca.

To Valerie Miles and Sandra Pareja, for encouraging me to believe that this book would, very soon, be read in other languages.

To Jon Lee Anderson and Alberto Salcedo Ramos, who lead the way, and whose stories mean I never forget what it means to be a reporter.

To Marco Avilés and Jeremías Gamboa, older brothers, and to Romina Mella, who watched my back in the final stretch by checking the facts.

To Stefanie Pareja, Diego Salazar, David Hidalgo, Toño Angulo, Agus Morales, Javier Sinay, Rodrigo Pedroso, Boris Muñoz and Sol Aliverti, who at different points and in different ways encouraged me to publish.

To Claudia Berríos, María Jesús Zevallos, Katery Morán, Giuliana Dávila and Julio Escalante, for their encouragement when this book was just the germ of an idea.

To Miguel Ángel Farfán, Richard Manrique and Walter Li, for every Day Three.

I would like to thank my family, especially my parents and siblings, who had to live without me for so long because I was travelling or shut away trying to write something that would move them.

And thank you to Rosa Chávez Yacila, who was able to tell me the truth and save me so many times from myself.